THE OAK ISLAND MYSTERY
– SOLVED –

JOY A. STEELE

THE OAK ISLAND MYSTERY
– SOLVED –

JOY A. STEELE

Cape Breton University Press
Sydney, Nova Scotia

Cape Breton University Press recognizes the support of Canada Council for the Arts and of the Province of Nova Scotia, through Film and Creative Industries NS, and we are pleased to work in partnership with these bodies to develop and promote our cultural resources.

Cover design: Cathy MacLean, Chéticamp, NS
Cover photo: From a photograph (copy) given to the author by Kaye Chappell, Sydney River, NS
Cover Illustration: Kaye Chappell, Sydney River, NS, inspired by Fig. 5.6.
Layout: Mike Hunter, Port Hawkesbury and Sydney, NS
First printed in Canada
Second printing 2016

Library and Archives Canada Cataloguing in Publication

Steele, Joy A., 1962-, author
    The Oak Island mystery, solved / Joy A. Steele.

Includes bibliographical references.
Issued also in print and electronic formats.
ISBN 978-1-77206-008-9 (pbk.).--ISBN 978-1-77206-009-6 (pdf).
--ISBN 978-1-77206-010-2 (epub).--ISBN 978-1-77206-011-9 (Kindle)

    1. Oak Island Treasure Site (N.S.)--History. 2. Treasure troves--Nova Scotia--Oak Island (Lunenburg)--History.
I. Title.

FC2345.O23S74 2015   971.6'23   C2015-901165-5
                                         C2015-901166-3

Cape Breton University Press
P.O. Box 5300
Sydney, NS B1P 6L2

The Oak Island Mystery – Solved

Table of Contents

Preface

A great deal has been recorded, written and published about the pursuit of treasure on Oak Island over the years – a great deal. I am certain that I've read it all in my own pursuit of the truth.

The purpose of this book is to share my research and, more important, that research with readers. I did not feel it necessary to reiterate the entire history of the pursuit of "Oak Island Gold." Those accounts are readily available in many forms, and the sources I have used are recounted in full in the references at the end of this book. For those wishing more detail of the many expeditions and explorations of Oak Island, I recommend the publications listed below.

I too pursued the Oak Island mystery. I hesitate to call my particular pursuit of the answer an obsession but, like so many others, I have taken it pretty seriously, though more interested in solving the mystery than in finding treasure. My education, indeed my interests, have long been in mineral technology and a number of the fascinating finds at Oak Island became the focus of my interest.

This book is the culmination of my pursuit of those clues. In a way, as the reader will learn, I did find treasure.

J.A.S.

Harris, Reginald V. 1967. *The Oak Island Mystery*, 2nd ed. Toronto: McGraw-Hill Ryerson.

Harris, Graham and Les MacPhie. 2005. *Oak Island And Its Lost Treasure*, 2nd ed. Halifax: Formac.

O'Connor, Darcy. 2004. *The Secret Treasure of Oak Island: The Amazing True Story of a Centuries-Old Treasure Hunt*. Guilford, CT: The Lyons Press.

Claudae C. Chappell – 1892-1980
(Photo courtesy Wendy Chappell)

This book is dedicated to the memory of Claude Chappell, a true pioneer and contributor to the history of Oak Island.

Many thanks are due to the Chappell family of Sydney, Nova Scotia, especially my dear friend, Kaye, who gave so much of herself to help me and whose painting is on the book cover. I am, in addition, very grateful to Catherine Arseneau, Jane Arnold and the crew at the Beaton Institute who went out of their way to lend a hand. A big thank you also goes out to Lisa Mulak and staff of the James McConnell Memorial Library in Sydney.

To Mike Harmon (archaeologist, South Carolina): You are a credit to your profession, and I will always be appreciative for your expertise and consultations.

I would also like to acknowledge the encouragement and support of Mike Hunter and the editorial staff of CBU Press.

Above all, I would like to thank my dear son, Christian, for his loving support and patience during the writing of this book. Mom will love you until the end of time.

Note from the Editors

As most of the history of, and activity on, Oak Island predates the use of metric in Canada, virtually every source consulted has measurements in feet, inches and miles, etc. – we have added their metric approximations.

We have made every effort to properly identify and to acquire the permissions to publish images, facts and figures. That's not always an easy task and, though every effort has been made to obtain those important aspects for this publicaation of Ms. Steele's research, we were not always successful. CBU Press understands and upholds its responsibilities in this regard to the best of our ability, and we sincerely regret possible infringements in this area.

Responsibility for the research and the opinions and theories proposed are the author's only.

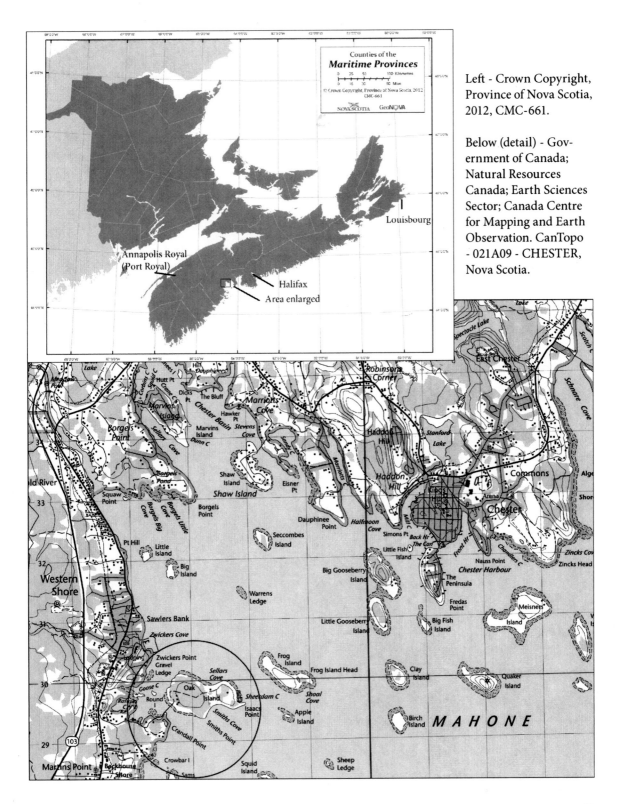

Left - Crown Copyright, Province of Nova Scotia, 2012, CMC-661.

Below (detail) - Government of Canada; Natural Resources Canada; Earth Sciences Sector; Canada Centre for Mapping and Earth Observation. CanTopo - 021A09 - CHESTER, Nova Scotia.

Introduction

The History and Folklore of Oak Island

Oak Island has become known as the most elusive treasure in the world, and the Money Pit and its adjacent works the greatest piece of engineering on the American continent. — R. V. Harris, The Oak Island Mystery

Fig. 1 – Newspaper feature from 1969 (*Sunday News*) highlighting the interest in Oak Island's buried treasure. "The Riddle of Oak Island," newspaper clipping, September 7, 1969. MG 12, 75 D3 (p. 10C). Beaton Institute, Cape Breton University.

1

Just off the rugged southeast shore of Nova Scotia lies a tiny island fashioned somewhat like a question mark. The shape is appropriate, for little Oak Island is the scene of a baffling whodunit that has defied solution for over two centuries. Here, since 1795 – not long after pirates prowled the Atlantic coast and left glittering legends of buried gold in their wake – people have been trying to find out what lies at the bottom of a mysterious shaft dubbed, hopefully, the Money Pit. (Reader's Digest, December 2014, 118-26)

Oak Island is one of more than 300 islands nestled within the confines of Mahone Bay, Nova Scotia. Situated about 6 km (4 miles) from Chester town, itself about 72 km (45 miles) southwest of Halifax, Oak Island measures approximately 1,200 m (.75 mile) in length and is about 800 m (.5 mile) wide, narrowing near the centre to form a low-lying marsh.

According to tradition, the current name, Oak Island, likely reflects a grove of lofty red oaks that once grew on the island's eastern drumlin.[1] These unique and impressive trees were not only the signature for the island but became part of its folklore as well. One creepy myth forewarns, "The treasure will be found … when all the oaks have gone and seven men have died."[2]

As if in fulfillment of the myth – or curse, as the case may be – the disturbing reality is that six men have died, thus far, in pursuit of an elusive treasure, and the oaks are all gone; their sad disappearance due largely to plagues of black ants in the 1800s, with the last few trees dying about 1960.[3]

Fig. 2 – Smith's Cove, Oak Island, ca. 1931. Note the majestic trees towering in the background along Isaac's Point. Photo (photographic copy) given to the author by Kaye Chappell, Sydney River, NS.

JOY A. STEELE

From the time of its "revelation" dating from the close of the 18th century, no less than seventeen expeditions have mounted attempts to overcome the island's challenges and to get to the bottom of the mystery, and thus to its treasure. So far, each attempt has ended in failure or disaster, collectively racking up costs in the millions of dollars. Worse still, of course, are the aforementioned lives lost in accidental deaths in the quest. Despite its violent history, the desire to unlock the island's secrets is alive and well as the current venture, Oak Island Tours Inc., establishes itself. This group suggests that it will be they who will provide the final chapter to this challenging and bizarre mystery spanning nearly 220 years. In fact, however, it will be this book that does that.

∞

So what is this enigma all about? Does the island really harbour a treasure? Is it the resting place of some ancient or holy relic? Is it a cache of priceless documents? The truth is that nobody really knows, and every imaginable theory, from the fantastic to the ridiculous, has been concocted to explain and uncover it. Most assuredly, treasure has been a powerful compulsion; entire fortunes and, as noted, lives have been risked and lost chasing empty or shattered dreams.

Whether a great mystery or a great scandal, the circumstances and events that surround this island are incredible, to say the least. In truth, the very root of the Oak Island story is embroiled with politics and treachery that rivals the intrigue of the treasure itself. Truly, this is the stuff of legends by which "history is made."[4]

To know the story of Oak Island is also to know how that story includes some very unsavoury behaviour, even by 18th-century standards, including what may have been the greatest financial scandal the world has ever witnessed.

Brief Chronology of Oak Island Events and Campaigns

1758 or 1759 – The island was without an English name, at this time. Numbered on maps as "Island 28."

1762 – Labelled as Smith's Island, named after Richard Smith on a map by Captain Charles Morris. Smith and partner, John Gifford, were granted this island on December 27, 1753, for the purpose of fishing.

1764 – First mention of Oak Island, as found in the diary of Reverend John Seccombe.

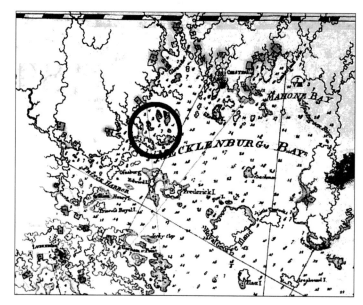

Fig. 3 – Map of Mecklenburgh Bay. (Detail) Southwest Coast of Nova Scotia, 1781. J.F.W. Desbarres. Map 1006. Beaton Institute, Cape Breton University.

1770s – Appears on Desbarres' *Neptune* maps as Gloucester Island, but came to be known once again and forever as Oak Island.

1795 – Daniel McGinnis allegedly first discovers a saucer-shaped depression on Oak Island's east drumlin. He and two friends, John Smith and Anthony Vaughn, began digging in the depression discovering a layer of flat stones 2 feet (60 cm) down, followed by a layer of oak timber at 10 feet (3 m). At 20 feet (6 m) another layer of oak timber is struck and, at 30 feet (10 m), more of the same. The trio are of the belief that Captain William Kidd (1645-1701) cached a treasure on the island not long before he was captured and hung for piracy.

1803-1805 – The Onslow Company is set up by Simeon Lynds of Truro along with the three discoverers McGinnis, Smith and Vaughn. Excavation of the so-called Money Pit continues and at around the 80-90-foot (24-27 m) level a stone inscribed with glyphs is found. They succeed in digging to 93 feet (28 m) but encounter flooding. The following year, a parallel shaft is dug to 110 feet (34 m) and then driven laterally toward the Money Pit. Within two feet of intersecting Money Pit, flooding again occurs.

1849-1851 – The Truro Company is formed and begins digging in the Money Pit. Water is encountered but operations resume, and they drill through what is assumed to be oak boxes containing metal in pieces, and then in a subsequent boring through cask(s) or barrels. The following year, further digging efforts are again frustrated by water problems. Attention switches to Smith's Cove when salty water is noticed issuing from shore banks. A quantity of coconut husks is discovered. A cofferdam is built and discovery is made of a complex system including box drains thought to be a system to flood the Money Pit.

1861-1864 – The Oak Island Association takes hold and begins work at the Money Pit, clearing down to 88 feet (27 m). A second parallel shaft is driven 25 feet (8 m) east of the Money Pit but abandoned. Another shaft is sunk 18 feet (5.5 m) west of the Money Pit and 118 feet deep (36 m). A lateral tunnel is then driven from its bottom intersecting the Money Pit. Flooding occurs and the Money Pit collapses. The partial end of a keg is noted among the debris. Later that year, the first life is claimed by Oak Island as an unidentified man is scalded to death by an exploding boiler.

1866-1867 – The Oak Island Eldorado Company (The Halifax Company) takes up work on the island in May. A cofferdam at Smith's Cove is constructed to investigate the filter bed and box drains but is shortly afterward destroyed by sea action. Efforts turn to the Money Pit and area, in vain. By late 1867 the company is dissolved.

1878 – The ground collapses beneath a team of oxen led by Sophia Sellers near Smith's Cove (350 feet (107 m) east of the Money Pit). Frederick L. Blair and searchers later dub the site the "Cave-in Pit."

1893-1900 – The Oak Island Treasure Company forms, led by Frederick L. Blair. In 1894, work begins with exploration of the Cave-in Pit but is cut short by water problems at a depth of 55 feet (17 m). Efforts switch back to the Money Pit, but stop due to flooding. In 1896, the company is restructured, and then work resumes at the Money Pit, eventually reaching the 97 foot mark (29.5 m). During this operation, on March 26, 1897, Maynard Kaiser falls to his death while being hoisted by rope from the Money Pit. Charges of dynamite are detonated near Smith's Cove in an effort to stem flooding in the Money Pit, in vain. The company continues to sink shafts and drill holes around the Money Pit area. A cement vault and a scrap of parchment are later discovered. A stone triangle formation is found on the south shore near the beach. Work continues in and around the Money Pit until finally halted due to flooding in 1900.

Fig. 4 – A young Franklin D. Roosevelt (third from the right) during a visit to Oak Island in 1909. From a book review of O'Connor, *The Money Pit* in *Business Week*, February 20, 1978, p. 10. MG 12, 75. Beaton Institute, Cape Breton University.

1909 – Old Gold Salvage and Wrecking Company decides to try their luck, led by Henry L. Bowdoin. Future United States President, Franklin D. Roosevelt, purchases stock in the company and turns up for several brief visits during that summer, working with Bowdoin's crew. A total of 28 holes are drilled in the vicinity of the Money Pit.

Fig. 5 right – Drilling rig on barge en route to the island. Unknown date, unknown photographer. Photo given to the author by Kaye Chappell.

Fig. 6 below – Busy assortment of people and buidlings at one of the workings. Unknown date, unknown photographer. Photo given to the author by Kaye Chappell.

Flooding, as well as funding problems, plague the enterprise and work stops by November 1909. Bowdoin then declares Oak Island a hoax.

1931 – Fred Blair and William Chappell are joined in this venture by: William Chappell's son, Mel; brother, Renwick, and nephew, Claude. A new pit is dug (the Chappell Shaft) just southwest of the Money Pit. Artifacts recovered included tools (probably a previous searcher's) and an anchor fluke embedded in clay (thought to be left by original builders). Mel Chappell eventually theorizes that a cache of priceless documents are the real treasure.

1934 – The Canadian Oak Island Treasure Company (Thomas Nixon of British Columbia, Canada) drilled fourteen holes over the summer and fall with no significant results. Frederick Blair terminates his contract on October 30 of the same year.

1936-1937 – Gilbert Hedden, in 1936, deepened the Chappell shaft to 160 feet (49 m). That same year, Hedden notices old timbers protruding from sand at Smith's Cove. A partial excavation reveals what is thought to be an old slipway. The following spring, Hedden sinks a shaft to 125 feet (38 m) near the northeast side of the Money Pit (the Hedden Shaft). The project is abandoned for lack of funds.

1938-1942 – Professor Erwin Hamilton undertakes to drill an additional fifty-eight holes down the Hedden shaft in 1938 finding nothing of great consequence. The next year he re-cribs the Chappell shaft to 160 feet (49 m). Hamilton returns to the Hedden shaft in 1940 and deepens a section to 155 feet (47 m). In 1941, he switches once again to the Chappell shaft and deepens it to 167 feet (51 m). The same year, he conducts dye tests showing a connection to deep water on the south shore. The project is closed due to an acute labour shortage as a result of the Second World War.

1955 – George Green drills four holes north of Chappell shaft finding little of any consequence. Green theorizes that a treasure was left by Spanish conquistadors during their conquest of Central and South America in the 16th century. (In 2014, another similar theory suggests that buried here is an Aztec treasure dating back to the 16th century.)[5]

1958 – Victor and William Harman conduct drilling in and around the Money Pit. Samples of oak, spruce and coconut fibre are brought up. Like George Green before them, the brothers believe a treasure was deposited by the Spanish. Insufficient finances causes the project to be terminated.

1960-1965 – Robert Restall, on a lease from Mel Chappell, explores the Money Pit and Hedden shafts. Extensive work is undertaken in the Smith's Cove area, digging sixty-five shallow pits and excavating two shafts. Part of the box drain system is unearthed during this time. Calamity strikes in August 1965, as Restall, his son, Bobbie, Cyril Hiltz and Karl Graeser die in a tragic accident on the island. Restall believed that a treasure was deposited by English privateers consisting of plunder from raids on Spanish ships and settlements during the 17th century.

1965-1966 – Robert Dunfield excavates at the south shore, the Money Pit and the Cave-in-Pit, and rediscovers the site of the original Money Pit. Heavy equipment does great destruction to the island, including the obliteration of the stone triangle.

1967-1969 – Dan Blankenship and David Tobias contract Becker Drilling Ltd., which sinks some sixty holes in and around the Money Pit. Core samples contained charcoal, oak buds, wood, cement, blue clay, metal and fragments of china. Excavations in Smith's Cove turn up many artifacts, including the remains of the box drain system, a heart-shaped stone, a metal ruler (or possibly a square set) and a pair of 300-year-old wrought iron scissors. Coconut fibre was also found.

Fig. 7 – Excavations inside the cofferdam exposed (lower centre) a u-shaped structure. Oak Island, 1970-1971. Photographer unknown. 81-576-5656. Beaton Institute, Cape Breton University.

1969-2005 – Triton Alliance Ltd. forms with Dan Blankenship and David Tobias and other investors. (Note that Triton Alliance had not held a board meeting since the mid 1990s but operated through wholly owned subsidiaries.) A cofferdam is built to probe more closely into Smith's Cove. The significant find of a u-shaped structure is excavated along with a wooden box. Golder and Associates of Toronto are hired to carry out an extensive geotechnical survey. Borehole "10X" is explored and later a shaft is sunk. Fragments of chain links and metal are collected. A camera lowered into the area shows grainy images of what is thought to be three chests.

1992 – Fred Nolan (independent landowner on Oak Island and treasure hunter) publicly announces his discovery of a megalithic stone Christian cross formed by five cone-shaped boulders (that he had found in 1981). At the intersection of the stem and arms was found an odd stone resembling a human skull. The cross measures 720 feet wide and 867 feet in length (219 by 264 m). Fred held the theory that the British military had buried a portion of the treasure plundered during the sack of Havana in 1762.

1995-1996 – The prestigious Woods Hole Oceanographic Institution is recruited, by Oak Island Discoveries Inc., to perform seismic, dye, side-scan sonar and piezometer tests in Smith's Cove, 10X and the Money Pit areas. Also done is detailed ground water, tomography and bathymetry mapping.[6]

2006-present – Oak Island Tours Inc. (along with Dan Blankenship) have resumed operations on the island with the goal of uncovering buried treasure and the mystery of Oak Island. Dan Blankenship's personal theory to date is that the island is a repository for gold and silver left behind by marauding Spaniards in the mid-16th century.

Fig. 8 – Illustration of Oak Island. Note the characterization of the island using a pirate motif. Newspaper feature from 1969 (*Sunday News*) that highlights the interest in Oak Island's buried treasure. (Detail) "The Riddle of Oak Island," newspaper clipping, September 7, 1969. MG 12, 75 D3 (p. C11). Beaton Institute, Cape Breton University.

Stories Told. Legends Born.

There have long-existed stories among the townsfolk of Chester about the "mysterious isle" just across the bay, tales of strange lights emanating from the island, of eerie voices carried across the water in the still of the night and of the alleged disappearance of two men who dared to investigate (ca. 1720). Did spirits inhabit the island? What sort of sinister activities took place there? The little isle came to be regarded with mistrust and fear.

Three young men – Daniel McGinnis, John Smith and Anthony Vaughn – were exploring the island sometime near the end of the 18th century, usually stated as 1795, as previously noted. An account in *The Colonist* in 1864, states that the Money Pit of Oak Island was discovered by McGinnis alone, and that he later called in the other two.[7] Understandably, renditions vary with the march of time but most agree in essence and with most quintessential facts of discovery. Suffice to say, the trio kindled the fires of imagination. Their discovery quickly became the talk of the town, creating an atmosphere charged with excitement and mystery and launching what is perhaps the world's greatest and longest running treasure hunt.

Edward Snow writes:

> In 1720 the people of the mainland had observed peculiar lights burning on Oak Island at night. Boatmen curious enough to cruise in the vicinity had seen the outlines of men believed to be pirates silhouetted against giant bonfires. Two fishermen who went to Oak Island to investigate did not return and were never heard from again. Finally the pirates, if such they were, disappeared from Mahone Bay and the area settled down to peace and quiet. But the women of Chester whose men had vanished never forgot the days when the pirates were active at Oak Island.... A feeling of terror toward the island had persisted ever since the 1720s.[8]

Oak Island became synonymous with buccaneers and tales inextricably intertwined with the romance of the sea, and buried treasure is part of that romance. There are many islands tucked in behind the larger offshore Tancook Islands affording both shelter and seclusion to mooring vessels. Mahone Bay – once called Mecklenburgh Bay and also Merligueche, among other names over the centuries according to tradition and conquest – was not only logistically an ideal location for buried treasure, but it really looked the part as well. Visitors in the early 1900s commented that Oak Island might well furnish as an illustration for *Treasure Island*, the classic novel by Robert Louis Stevenson (1883).

Few would say that the island is just one of many similar islands along this coast; this was the only island in the whole bay with lofty oak trees, giants that were leafy only toward their tops, towering like palm umbrellas. The presence of the oaks, it was said, "lent the place an eerie air, even in mid-morning."[9] Often, a creepy mist shrouds the island, adding to the mystique, swirling over the footpaths like the entrails of a ghostly phantom hand. To some folks, even the island's shape brings to mind that of an old cutlass, curving to its eastern extremity and making for a sheltered cove for sea landings.

Longstreth Interview

The following is one rendition of the discovery story as recorded by author T. M. Longstreth in his book *To Nova Scotia* (1935),[10] in which he wrote of an interview with an unnamed Chester woman. Unnamed perhaps in a desire to preserve her anonymity:

Informant:

"The location, as you must admit," she began, "might well have appealed to buccaneers. Once inside the Tancooks, a privateer could take his time hunting a suitable place. And even if the rumor got around that treasure was being buried on one of the islands, there are enough of them to make searching for the proper one right tiresome. There are 365 islands, you know."

Longstreth: (I generously made no comment).

Informant:

"It was in that cove where you landed that three young men chanced to land in 1795. The Island was uninhabited, of course, but they noticed that some of the ground had been cleared years before, and red clover and other plants unusual to the soil were growing there. The young men were still more surprised to find a big oak in the clearing with one of its lower limbs sawn off. It looked as if this stump had accommodated a heavy block and tackle. Beneath was a circular depression some 13 feet across [4 m]."

Longstreth: "Excuse me," I said, "but are we still on fact or have we launched into surmise?"

Informant:

"These are facts. I'm going to tell you only facts. You can do your own surmising. The whole shore came to know these things, and there's a great iron ring-bolt imbedded in a rock and visible only at low tide, which the young men discovered at the same time. It can still be seen. They picked up a copper coin, dated 1713, as well as a boatswain's stone whistle, a kind which even then had gone out of use.

The three of them began digging, of course, as soon as they could fetch tools without stirring up suspicion, and they uncovered a sort of well. At ten feet [3 m] down they came to a covering of oak plank. At twenty feet [6 m] a second covering. And at thirty [10 m] a third. But it's no fun hauling dirt up thirty feet [10 m], so they tried to get help. Either the neighbors had no faith in the well then, or were too busy, for nobody would help, and after a little more digging the young men gave it up."

Longstreth: "They had avarice well in hand," I could not help but saying.

Informant:

"Well, six years went by and then a Doctor Lynds of Truro got up a company to continue the search. The shaft was cleared [down] to 95 feet [29 m] with marks being found every ten feet [3 m] on the way down. One of them was a layer of cocoanut [sic] fiber. It was a Saturday evening that the diggers struck a wooden platform at the 95-foot level and they had to stop. People were God-fearing in those days and respected the Sabbath. But when they went back on Monday morning, the shaft was found filled with water to within 25 feet [7.5 m] of the top."

Longstreth: "It sounds true," I murmured.

Informant:

"They tried baling [sic], of course, but that was useless. So they sank a new shaft to the east of the Money Pit, as the first well had got to be called. They sank it 110 feet [33 m] without reaching water. But then, while they were driving a tunnel towards the Money Pit, water burst in and nearly drowned some of the diggers.

This second disaster ended things. The pits filled up and the men in Lynds's company died. But the notion that there was money there didn't die. Finally in 1849, when only two of the old-timers were left, a new company was got up. They located the Money Pit and got down 85 feet [26 m] before water drove them out. Then they rigged a platform and began boring with an apparatus used in prospecting for coal. I've still got a copy of the manager's report around somewheres, if you'd like to see it."

Longstreth:

...I asked to see the paper. It was fascinatingly circumstantial. The treasure-seekers had bored through a layer of wood found at 98 feet down [30 m]. After penetrating five inches [12 cm] of spruce and four [10 cm] of oak, the augur bit into metal, in pieces, but failed to take any of it except three links resembling ancient watch-chain. After twenty-two inches [55 cm] of treasure came eight inches [20 cm] of oak and a second twenty-two inches of metal as before. Then clay. They had gone through the hoard.

The story now grew more complicated. There was treachery at directors' meetings, and more shaft-sinking. It was noted that the water in the pit rose and fell with the tide. So part of the shore was shoveled away and a blanketing of brown fibrous plant was discovered over a system of rock drains. A coffer dam was built and swept away by a storm. The Money Pit caved in.

The shipping boom now brought visible treasure to Nova Scotia and the invisible was forgotten.... But not entirely. A new company with a capital of $60,000 brought pumps and steam engine and cook-house and offices to Oak Island. The pirate tunnel was sought in the belief that if it could be blocked, then the Pit could be dug out once more and the hoard hoisted finally to the light of day. But to no avail.

Informant: "They spent their sixty thousand, and others after them have spent more. Nearly a quarter of a million has been run through going after that treasure."

Longstreth: "And what do you think?" I asked my informer.

"She hasn't told you all she knows," spoke up her husband promptly.

Informant: "No, there are things one isn't at liberty to speak about," she sighed.

Longstreth: "So, I gathered from the current adventurers," I said, rising. "Meanwhile I thank you for a very mystifying evening."[11]

∞

As any die-hard Oak Island enthusiast can tell you, bizarre history, weird happenings and new twists around every corner are just part of the lore they have come to know. When bad luck occurs or something new or strange happens on the island, folks pretty much shrug it off and chalk it up to all things Oak Island. But without exception, and by far, the strangest episodes of the island's history are presented in the following three tales. No Hollywood yarn could match the first two stories for bravery and pluck – yet, they are true. They took place right on Oak Island. These and other sea stories and tales embody, for me, the island's creepier side.

Borehole 10X

"And each man said, 'damn, that's a hand … that's a human hand'!!" – Daniel Blankenship.

Coming into existence as a mere 6-inch exploratory drill hole (15 cm) commissioned by Triton during the summer of 1970, borehole 10X – called as such for its location on a survey grid plan – is some 180 feet (55 m) northeast of the so-called Money Pit. For Triton partner, Dan Blankenship, 10X quickly became a sweet spot begging to be exploited to the fullest. There were far too many clues of past human involvement turning up to let such an area alone. It turned out that there were things in chasms below that would cause anyone to rub their eyes in disbelief. For Dan Blankenship, 10X marks a dangerous spot where he once cheated death.

Fig. 9 – Two of four images on a scrapbook page describing Triton's drilling on the island. Pictured at left is a Keystone 50 drill, which could bore a hole up to 16 in (40 cm) diameter, 600 ft (183 m) deep. Below, is a photo of a piece of wire found in a clay core sample. Tests proved that the wire, 0.125 in (32 mm) by 2 in (5 cm) long, was made from low-carbon steel between 1500 and 1800 CE. Oak Island, July 1973. Photographer unknown. 81-541-5621. Beaton Institute, Cape Breton University.

Promising results were quickly turned up from the test hole, making it clear at the onset that this was to be a site of some interest. Underground voids or cavities were struck at three levels, beginning near the 140-foot level and extending down to a depth of around 230 feet (43-70 m). Blown topside from the drill from 165 feet (50 m) came odd slivers of thin metal which, at first, held the appearance and colour of lead, but then began to oxidize and turn brittle within moments. Rapid oxidation is characteristic of certain metals when in an oxygen-deprived state for some time. More discoveries followed: chain links, wire and sections of angular steel. Samples were sent on to Stelco Steel Company for analysis, hoping to shed some light about the artifacts. Amazingly, the metal scraps and chain were determined to predate the

year 1750 and found to be composed of an early form of smelted low-carbon steel.

Encouraged by the results, the Triton team chose to widen the shaft and send down an underwater video camera for closer inspection – unprepared for the gruesome sight about to greet them. While three men manned the equipment outside, Dan monitored the screen from a nearby shack. As the camera came to rest at around the 230-foot mark (70 m), the first images were beamed back to the surface. At first there was stark silence, then a blood-curdling yelp from the shack. One by one each of the four men were called in to view the bizarre spectacle which hovered eerily before them.

Dan recalls, "I didn't say anything and just pointed to the screen. And each man said, 'damn, that's a hand ... that's a human hand'!!" The image of a severed and partly clenched human hand later described by Dan as appearing "to be floating in perfect equilibrium in the water." To this day Dan swears it was a hand he saw, "right down to the fingernails," and no amount of time or talk will ever persuade him otherwise. He was once quoted as saying, "Now I don't say I think I saw a hand in there. I don't say that. I saw a hand. There's no question about it."[12]

The impression left on Dan would last a lifetime. His old curiosities about 10X have never left him. On November 25, 1976, he allowed himself to be lowered deep into the bowels of 10X to get a look at things first hand. Engineers had been by a few days prior to inspect the casing and declared it to be quite safe – but there was terrible danger lurking below.

Dan's son, David, was among the crew on hand that day – he too was about to become part of Oak Island lore. Every four hours or so, he and Dan took turns between operating the winch and going down the shaft. On this occasion, it would be David's turn at the winch hoisting his father in and out of the shaft.

Dan was lowered to a depth of 95 feet (29 m) to a spot that he had, just days before, identified as an area of interest. Preliminary finds indicated the presence of a cavity in the earth just beyond the casing, so window-like sections were cut out in an effort to gather more visual details. Now, as he dangled in front of that spot, he found that it was too choked off by silt and debris to get a good look into whatever lay behind. The area would need to be cleaned and flushed out, and he no sooner said the words, "I'm going to get nothing but a face full of mud—" when he began to feel pieces of earth dropping on him from somewhere above.

"You're going to have to bring me up a bit. Now bring me up another foot please," Dan's voice crackled through the radio transmitter to David. It was then that all hell broke loose, literally, as rubble began

Fig. 10 – The piece of casing that nearly crushed Dan Blankenship. Courtesy of the author.

to barrel freely down the shaft from just overhead. Suddenly, David could hear the frantic screams of his father as he shouted, "BRING ME UP; BRING ME UP; OUT, OUT, OUT, OUT, OUT, OUT, OUT, OUT, OUT, OUT!!!

David found himself staring down what must have looked and sounded like a hole to hell – his father screaming as the shaft began to implode in a cacophony of horror. Rocks and debris plunged down the shaft, pummelling Dan in the process. David had to think and work fast; death had its claws out ready to claim another victim on Oak Island.

The screaming continued, "I'M OK, BRING ME OUT, OUT, OUT. I'M OK; BRING ME OUT, BRING ME OUT, BRING ME OUT, BRING ME OUT. I'M OK; KEEP BRINGING ME OUT, BRING ME OUT; DON'T STOP; BRING ME UP; IT'S STILL OVER MY HEAD [the debris that's falling]; OVER MY HEAD; BRING ME UP.

At this point, panic and pressure would have been overwhelming enough for anybody, but knowing his own father's life rested in his hands must have been especially unnerving for 26-year-old David. Had he not kept the gas-powered winch revved up, it surely would have stalled leaving Dan to be crushed like a bug in a soda can. But he did not falter, safely gliding his father above the trouble spot. Upon reaching the sanctity of the surface, Dan said, somewhat endearingly, "Don't tell your mother David, my God," as if the scolding was feared more than the sin.

In September of 2011, it was my great pleasure on a visit to Oak Island to chat with Dan; of course, I was hoping to glean a bit more detail about his near-fatal experience. I have always adored talking to the gentleman, as Oak Island is a beloved topic of discussion for us both. He was hovering over a crock of beans when I arrived, and I couldn't help but think at the time how energetic and vibrant a soul he still was. He once signed a copy of a book for me, "always keep trying"; inspiring words I came to live by, as at the time I was slugging it out in a battle with cancer.

At one point, he looked me straight in the eye and said, "I would never ask anybody to do what I had done," reminiscing about his dangerous trials and tribulations on the island. Of his son, David, who had in fact saved his life, his comments were particularly touching. Fatherly pride radiated from his eyes as he told me from the heart that, "he had sense enough to rev up the engine, because if you didn't, it would have died. He's proven to me that he keeps his head when the average person would lose their concentration. His reaction time was very quick, and still, he put thinking into it. He does not procrastinate."

It occurred to me that Dan Blankenship had found a treasure – new-found love and respect for his son in a time of crisis.

THE ED WHITE STORY

"I just couldn't go away and let him die...."

August 17, 1965, started out sticky and humid, typical of the sultry summer weather for that time of year on Mahone Bay. On Oak Island's northeast side, at Smith's Cove, Robert Restall and his crew were busy drilling. "Bob," as most called him, had worked and suffered chasing the treasure dream for the better part of six years. His expectations were high, for he was known to have commented during those last days that he was on the verge of unearthing the hoard.

His chance to hunt treasure on Oak Island, and fulfill his dreams, had come in 1959 when he successfully entered into an agreement with M. R. Chappell (owner of most of Oak Island at that time). Shortly afterward, Restall and his then 18-year-old son, Bobby, moved to the island and set up a humble residence. They were followed by his wife, Mildred, and youngest boy, Ricky. Eventually, crew members – most of them friends – joined him in his work of exploration, including Karl Graeser, a mineralogist from Massapequa, New York, who invested some money in the venture. Cyril Hiltz and Andrew DeMont, local lads both age sixteen, were also hired to the Restall team.

Restall had been concentrating his efforts on cutting off the so-called flood tunnels believed to be on the site, which he considered an essential first step in retrieving the treasure. Near the entrance of a supposed flood tunnel from Smith's Cove to the Money Pit, he sank a shaft 27 feet in depth (8 m). On the surface, a gasoline-powered pump was in use, spewing out carbon monoxide fumes as it chugged along.

Meanwhile, on the nearby mainland, a vacationing firefighter from New York state, Edward J. White, and his family had just hired a Cape Islander to ferry them over to the island. Ever since Mrs. White read about the mystical isle in *Reader's Digest*,[13] she had been fascinated by the stories of treasure and valuables said to be concealed there. It was at her urging that they planned to pay a visit to Oak Island as they passed through Nova Scotia. It is not hard to imagine the excitement of being in the proximity of a treasure and suppose that, at any moment, the earth might heave up the riches before their very eyes. The Whites were certainly in for excitement that day, but they could never have imagined the form it would take.

On the island, the Restall family was preparing for a trip to town. The next part is not entirely clear, but it would appear that Robert may have been taking a last minute look into the shaft or had climbed down into the pit, when he was overcome by some noxious and poisonous gas emission. He tumbled unconscious into the depths of the very pit he was working.

Bobby, who was gathering brush with three workmen nearby, realized something was wrong and rushed to the site. His frantic cry for help could be heard just before he climbed into the shaft to save his father. Friend and partner, 38 year-old Karl Graeser, followed next in response to Bobbie's cries for help. Without hesitation, Graeser scrambled to descend the ladder. Right behind him rushed young Cyril Hiltz, determined to help. Cyril's cousin, Andrew DeMont, a tall and strong young man of only sixteen, followed. When Andrew reached the bottom, only Bobby Jr. and Cryil were there alive; Restall (Sr.) and Graeser had succumbed to the noxious gas. Andrew must have known there was no going back up and soon lost consciousness.

It was reported that two others entered the shaft but escaped before being overcome, which correlates with the White family's report of seeing two such men in another boat while on their way to Oak Island.

Not far away, Peter Beamish and a group of students in the vicinity at the time had caught wind of Bobby's cries for help and raced toward the scene. Unaware of the drama unfolding, it was at about this time the White family had left the mainland and were heading toward Smith's Cove. They had picked up an additional passenger when a fellow at Western Shore learned a boat was headed to Oak Island and wanted to go there as well. As the island drew nearer, excitement hung in the air for the family, but the anticipation changed to horror.

En route to the island, the Whites encountered an oncoming boat which seemed to be heading straight at them. The White's pilot veered away, but the other craft manoeuvred toward them and it became obvious that they wanted to communicate. Something was afoot but, probably not wishing to cause panic, the other boat driver simply said to the unknown passenger, "they were looking for you over there." Then he motioned to two fellows who were huddled together pitifully on a seat in the boat and in an apparent state of shock. They had somehow managed to escape the pit but were in need of medical attention.

After a brief conversation not intended for the tourists' ears, for whatever reason the extra passenger in Sawlers' craft then changed boats to return to shore with the distressed men, and the White family and their driver continued on toward the tragedy unfolding at Smith's Cove. As they made their approach into the cove, a curious cluster of several men could be seen milling around a platform covering a portion of the shaft and looking down into it. It turns out, they had just lowered a rope and were desperately trying to rescue others apparently trapped below.

Figure 11 – Ed White. Photo courtesy of Ed White Jr.

It didn't take Ed White long to recognize that the scene playing out in front of him was likely a case of serious gas poisoning. He explained that he was trained in rescue, and situations like these were not new to him. He was a professional firefighter back home in New York, and had been involved in numerous rescue attempts during the course of his career. He set about fashioning a secure hitch in a rope given him by the other men. He tied the rope around his upper legs and armpits in a manner that would prevent him from becoming inverted in the event he somehow lost control.

As he was fastening the rope hitch around himself, his wife stood facing him. Their eyes met as she peered tearfully into his, knowing what he was about to do. "Edward you have a wife and three children," she pleaded, knowing in her heart that it was pointless to try and stop him. She acquiesced and led their two younger sons out of harm's way.

Ed put the rope in his oldest son's hands (Ed junior) and instructed him not to pull him out of the pit unless signalled to do so. He was assisted by other courageous volunteers who had gathered around – Richard Barder, James Keizer, Peter Beamish and others. Ed, with a second coil of rope over his shoulder, gulped a lungful of air and made his way down into oblivion, determined to cheat death.

Ed descended into the pit, carefully and methodically climbing down the cribbing on the shaft walls, presumably to conserve oxygen. At this point, even the creases in Ed's neck and underarms began to hurt and ache like bee-stings as sweat mixed with the caustic gas now engulfing his body.

Reaching the murky waters of the pit below, there in a corner he spied a pitiable sight – a man desperately clutching the cribbing, only his head exposed between the surface of the murky water and a horizontal log. It was Andrew DeMont, now alone above the surface. Black water rushed into his mouth as he alternatively vomited and breathed, all the while emitting a ghastly rasping noise that echoed up the shaft to the horror of all above.

Ed knew this man was close to death and that he needed to hurry. Only then did he remember that he had just recently cracked a rib and briefly pondered how in the world he would ever manage. The man in front of him – whose name he would later learn was Andrew – while still in a state of delirium, threw a weak punch at Ed, missing, but compounding matters. The men at the top of the pit had mistaken the scuffle as a signal that Ed was in danger and, hence, pulled his rope tight, ready to haul him up.

Until now, Ed was able to hold his breath, but when he yelled up for the men to stop, he inadvertently swallowed the foul air which nearly caused him to choke. He must have thought he had climbed straight into hell. As he looked upward, he saw what looked to him like a greenish-yellow haze contrasting with the skyline above the mouth of the shaft. Nevertheless, he was able to keep his composure and harness the now unconscious Andrew with the second rope, under both arms, between his legs and secured upright behind his head. The signal was given and Andrew's limp body was quickly hoisted up the shaft.

Still determined to find the earlier victims, Ed stayed back and continued to grope around, desperately plunging his arm down into the water as deep as it would go without putting his face under. This last-ditch effort was mercilessly in vain, however, for at this point Ed himself was running out of breath and at risk of passing out. No alternative was left to him except to try and make it back to the surface, which he did, managing to crawl up that hole under his own steam, unmended rib and all. It was nothing short of miraculous how he made it back, but he did, having given a young man another chance at life in the process.

Upon reaching the safety of the surface, Ed instructed the others to wrap Andrew in plenty of blankets, fearing the onslaught of shock. Spent and with skin burning, a soaking wet Ed and his son walked stoically over to a nearby log to rest and recover from the ordeal. His wife and sons rushed to his side, peppering him with hugs and overjoyed that he was safe and unharmed. Things could have come out a lot differently that day, they knew, and they counted their many blessings.

Not long afterward, firemen from Chester had the sad duty of recovering the bodies of Karl Graesar, Cyril Hiltz, Robert and Bobby Restall. Onlookers from the mainland reported that a strange fog had, at that time, moved in and enveloped only the island – all around remained strangely clear – appearing to all like an eerie funeral pall had been thrown over the tiny isle from the heavens themselves.

Regarding the treasure, it remained Robert Restall's firm belief, right up until the time of his death, that he was "within a few feet of its discovery," and that just four or five more days of work would result in him striking pay dirt. In a chillingly prophetic statement, Robert remarked that he was "not leaving the island without that treasure."

Many accounts of the tragedy point the finger at the poisonous carbon monoxide fumes emitted from the pump as being the cause of the accident. However, carbon monoxide is lighter than air, and the pump motor was positioned on a tripod on a platform several feet above the shaft in open air. It is noteworthy that some on the scene that day reported a foul odour, like rotten eggs, and that this stench clung to the clothes they wore for days afterward. This is usually indicative of another potentially deadly culprit – hydrogen sulphide gas (H_2S), perhaps the product of a ruptured gas pocket. Others point to the greenish-yellow cloud Ed described as he looked from the tunnel toward the opening above, suggesting that it may have been chlorine gas. Reportedly, there were other witnesses who, at other times, spoke of seeing greenish bubbles coming from the bottom of the pit. The distinct possibility remains that Mr. Restall and the others met their demise as a result of either gas or even a toxic cocktail of gases.

Two days after the tragedy, Ed White wrote down the events while the horrific facts still dwelled in his mind, ending his letter with the heart-wrenching avowal – "I just couldn't go away and let him die...." Later that year, in 1965, Mr. White was awarded the Medal of Bravery by the Canadian government in appreciation for his exceptional courage for saving another, even though his own life was in mortal danger. He was also honoured back at home in Buffalo, NY, with a second medal for heroism from his fire department at their annual firefighter's dinner.

Sadly, Captain Ed White passed away in 1972, stricken with cancer. A sorry loss. The people of Nova Scotia should never forget this man of rare courage.

Paranormal Oak Island

Local folks probably won't argue with you much if you claimed supernatural forces were at work on Oak Island; there have been countless reports of spectres and spirits prowling about there throughout the years. Even visions of a great ghostly conflagration and disembodied animal spirits have been reported by many different people, including some people I have known for years.

One of the strangest tales comes from Dan Henskee, who was at one time Dan Blankenship's full-time assistant. The story was recorded by author Darcy O'Connor. Henskee was a man that relished the solitary life as much as the lore of Oak Island, and so it was that in 1982, he took up residence on the island, living in a lonely shack positioned atop the Money Pit. One evening in 1995, he suffered a dreadful experience which nearly frightened him to death, a horrifying vision that so terrified him that he plunged naked into the channel and swam frantically to the nearby mainland. Curious as to what Mr. Henskee may have witnessed, I enquired of him what he had seen that evening that so frightened him. He divulged to me that he had envisioned the Money Pit as the mouth to hell, spewing "demons and such" from the depths below. He offered no further details.

Dan Blankenship once passed an eerie comment to writer D'Arcy O'Connor as if summing up the issue, saying, "Dan [Henskee] has paid a hell of a price for being involved with Oak Island, because he saw what I know is still down there in those tunnels."[14]

Author John O'Brien recounts the time he and a friend were camped on an Oak Island beach, taking shelter under an overturned dory. According to O'Brien, they heard footsteps on the gravel beach nearby. The footsteps approached their shelter, then "next to the boat, they stopped. [A]fter what seemed an eternity, the footsteps retreated towards the beach. The normal sounds of the night returned." Investigating, they found nothing – no tracks in the sand or gravel, nothing to give them a clue as to what they had just experienced. They made a hasty and fearful retreat from the island in the leaky old boat.[15]

∞

Another famous and bizarre tale from the island is one about little Peggy Adams, an innocent five-year-old who lived on Oak Island in her childhood years (ca. 1939-1945). There are still some ruins of their home visible atop the little knoll which flanks the road to the pit to the southeast. This account was related to me by her brother, George, who I met while on a tour of Oak Island in 2010. As fate would have it, I found myself at the right place and time on Oak Island when I had a chance meeting with George, then a man in his eighties. He was a delight to chat with, and it wasn't hard to sense his deep connections with the island. After speaking with George, I penned the following from memory of the visit.

The story goes that Peggy, just a wee girl back in 1940, had run in from play, frightened and crying about "three big men" she saw lurking about at nearby Smith's Cove. The tale grew stranger, as the child spoke about one of the men as having dark skin, while describing the others in the military attire of a bygone era. Peggy's father dispatched himself at once to the cove where he was sure he would see their tracks, as fresh snow had recently blanketed the island. But, neither track nor trace could be found to corroborate the youngster's claim, although according to George, Peggy, now in her seventies, still stands fast on what she saw.

Her story doesn't end there; a few years later, while visiting the Citadel Museum in Halifax, Peggy's mother once again found herself astonished. Evidently, an old uniform on display there was a dead ringer for the description Peggy had provided years earlier: "They were wearing pretty red jackets and had big yellow stripes down their pants," Peggy had proclaimed. The problem is, you see, that style of clothing and uniforms which the little girl professed to have seen were in fashion in the 1700s, more than 200 years previous. For one so young to have spoken about and described the clothing in such detail was just plain uncanny, if not impossible. Peggy is just one of the many who have said to have had a vision of "God only knows what" from some distant past on Oak Island.[16]

Whether or not the paranormal is at work on the island is debatable for some – less so for skeptics – but it is very difficult to deny that the spiritual side has become part of the lore. Author D'Arcy O'Connor once wrote of a particularly interesting comment on the subject from an unnamed elderly descendant of Anthony Vaughn's (one of the earliest discoverers of the Money Pit). With his statement came assurances that he would never set a foot on Oak Island, explaining:

> Weird as it may sound, I've seen people there; but not solid people. Ghosts. I've seen them from my property, from when I was a boy right up till now. They're ghosts, just wandering around, waiting for something ... or for somebody.[17]

∞

And so it went with each venture that attempted to unlock the mystery and to recover a lost treasure. The story grew like the web of a spider; woven and spun adding a new twist here and another part there – and, like a web, capturing the imagination of many great men and women who sought to unravel her secrets. From the likes of actors John Wayne and Errol Flynn to curious politicians, including Franklin D. Roosevelt and former Canadian Prime Minister Pierre Elliott Trudeau, all held in common a burning curiosity – an obsession for some – wrought by the ever-enlarging legend. This is the spell cast by the unresolved mystery of Oak Island, but the greatest story has yet to be told. Until now.

So much for spectres and speculation. Now, it is necessary to reflect more thoroughly and less romantically on past history and facts. On to solving the mystery, for indeed the reader will find that the truth of Oak Island will vary vastly from conventional thought about its secrets.

Part One – Pieces of the Puzzle

The so-called Money Pit has been the subject of much debate and provoked much controversy since its discovery in the late 18th century. Millions of dollars have been expended (and six lives lost) in anticipation of spectacular rewards – treasure or other worldly riches, including an Aztec treasure.[1] Others have speculated that the Oak Island works may have been something of a more holy nature, perhaps built as a booby-trapped repository housing holy relics.[2] No matter what dizzying height the imagination climbed to or whatever theory was imagined or conceived, the timeless obsession of treasure hunting synonymous with Oak Island prevails. People, including me, could hardly be blamed for straying a little toward the fantastic; it wasn't as if there weren't plenty of distortions and intimations to induce delusions of grandeur and riches.

Fig 1.1 – Ground depression near the site of the original Money Pit, ca. 2010. Photo courtesy of the author.

The puzzle, and the desire to put it together, starts with McGinnis, Smith and Vaughn's observation of a depression in the ground during that outing on the island in 1795.

First Impressions - The Money Pit

It's interesting how the moniker, Money Pit, has become the de facto name for all subsequent explorations.

Judge Mather DesBrisay (*History of the County of Lunenburg*), gives probably one of the best early accounts of discovery in which is stated that a tier of flagstones were unearthed by the lads about 2 feet (60 cm) below the surface of a depression they encountered. They afterward ascertained that the stones were not indigenous to the island and were believed to have been harvested from the vicinity of the nearby Gold River, two miles distant, and subsequently transported to Oak Island.[3]

That the pit they uncovered was later found to contain a number of rather unusual objects added to speculation about secret priceless booty: a bizarrely inscribed stone, for one (see more below). The Onslow group had pulled it up in 1804[4] from around the 80-90-foot (24-27 m) level and, subsequently, it was witnessed by many to have borne some unintelligible

Fig. 1.2 – Money Pit boldly circled. Oak Island-Topographical Map, 1934. S. Edgar March. MG 12.175 D.2A. Beaton Institute, Cape Breton University.

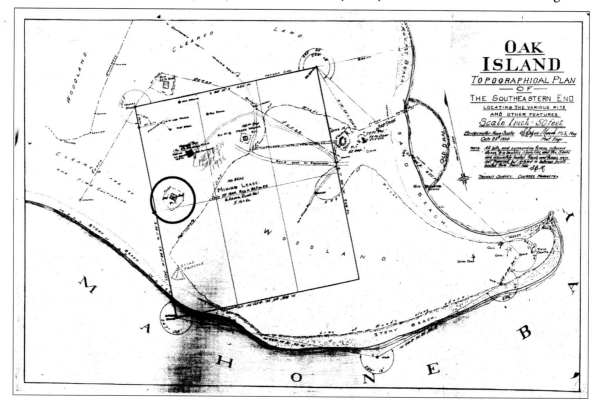

glyphs. As if that wasn't enough to conjure up fantasies of treasure and fortune, in 1897, a wee scrap of velum parchment, bearing what appeared to be handwritten script, was recovered at the 47 m (153 foot) mark (see more below).

Many dispel the inscribed stone and parchment as objects of folly; even as hoaxes designed to bait potential investors. However, in light of new research these items take on a different lustre and our purpose is only momentarily distracted by the Money Pit.

A point of keen interest about the Money Pit are the reports that at each and every 10 feet (3 m) lay a tier of oak logs. If one goes back to the original records describing the Money Pit, however, it is stated that only three layers of logs at ten-foot (3-m) intervals were observed by the three lads after discovery. In a letter to the *Yarmouth Herald* (July 10, 1862), J. B. McCully of the Oak Island Association lets us know that after the Onslow Company took up the work on Oak Island, "they commenced where they [the 3 lads] first left off, and sunk the pit 93 feet [28 m], finding a mark every 10 feet [3 m]. – Some of them were charcoal, some putty, and one at 80 feet [24 m] was a stone cut square...."

Inscribed Stone

Since its discovery more than 200 years ago, investigators and researchers have been intrigued by the mysterious stone – or at least by the anecdotes ascribed to it – uncovered from the Money Pit during excavation, and its supposed message to would-be treasure hunters. The stone has unfortunately been lost to us, lending some to doubt its veracity, that of its message or of having a message at all. Some are of the belief that the stone and its inscription truly existed, but over the course of time got swapped out and replaced with a fake.

The inscribed stone was first discovered around the 80-foot-level (24 m) in the Money Pit in 1804 by the Onslow Company.[5] The first known newspaper account of an inscribed stone, albeit brief, was actually in the *Halifax Sun and Advisor*, dated July 2, 1862, written by J. B. McCully, secretary of the Oak Island Association. In that description of the excavation ca. 1803-1805, McCully makes this fleeting mention of the stone stating that, "at 80 feet was a stone cut square, two feet long and about a foot thick, with several characters cut on it."[6]

At some point within the next few years, John Smith (one of the original discoverers of the Money Pit) gained possession of the stone and proceeded to install it into his fireplace during construction of his new

Fig. 1.3 – Replica of the "inscribed stone" commissioned by author Darcy O'Connor, in the mid 1980s, for a television documentary drama for the ABC network.[7] Photo courtesy Darcy O'Connor. Shared with the author and published with permission.

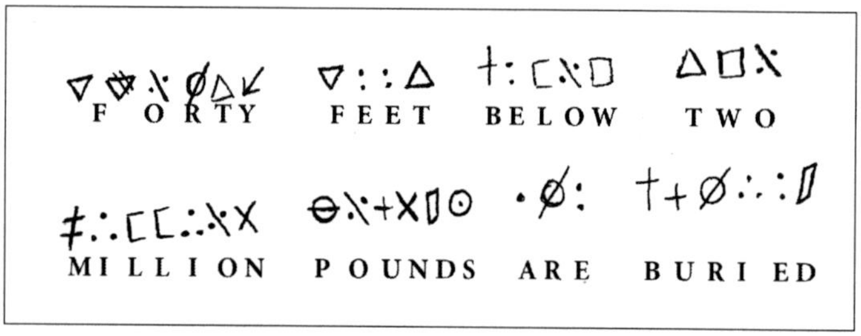

Fig. 1.4 – The glyphs as rendered by A. T. Kempton in an unpublished manuscript, recorded by Richard Joltes, overlaid with the widely accepted decoded message. NSARM. Kempton, A. T., story about Oak Island (typescript) Apr 28 1949. R. V. Harris Papers MG 1 vol 384, item 2364f-h.

home on Oak Island (ca. 1810). There the stone curio remained, admired and safe for 55 years.

In 1849, a new group was formed to take up the challenge of recovering the elusive treasure. The new venture was to be known as the Truro Company, named as such for the town where many of the members were born. Daniel McGinnis had unfortunately passed away by this time and, sometime in the month of August in 1857, John Smith also died.[8] Two out of three of the original discoverers of the Money Pit were gone, leaving only Anthony Vaughn.

Smith's property was afterward acquired by Anthony Graves and the old homestead put to use as a headquarters for the Truro Company, and then, subsequently, by the Oak Island Association. Evidently, neither seemed to realize that the inscribed stone was right in front of them; snugly embedded in John Smith's old fireplace.

On January 2, 1864, another mention of the stone's whereabouts is published in the Halifax *British Colonist*. In this instance, we are assured that the stone remained nestled and as yet undisturbed within Smith's fireplace. Although the update was by an anonymous writer toward the end of 1863, the article indisputably notes that, "As it was preserved in the family of Mr. Smith, it may be seen by the curious at the present day."[9] Within a year or two however, the stone was removed again.

There is some confusion as to where next the stone made its travels. According to author Charles Driscoll, it was taken to the Truro home of J. B. McCully. There, Driscoll claims, it was exhibited to hundreds of friends for some time.

R. V. Harris, in his book, *The Oak Island Mystery* (1967), states that sometime within 1865-1866 the stone was removed once again and taken to Halifax. Among others, a Mr. Jefferson W. MacDonald was one of those who worked to remove the stone from John Smith's fireplace. Mr. MacDonald told Frederick Blair in 1894 that "the inscription was easily traced but that no person present could decipher it."[10]

At some point, all reports agree that the stone appears to have ended up in the hands of bookbinder, A. O. Creighton in Halifax, brought there by either himself or Herbert Creighton. The former was treasurer of the Oak Island Association. The stone was prominently exhibited in their shop window, at a time when the company was endeavouring to sell shares to the public.

According to the information contained in the prospectus of the Oak Island Treasure Company, either the stone itself, or more likely a rubbing, appears to have gone out to an expert for translation purposes. His reading of the inscription was interpreted to be "ten feet below are two million pounds buried." (Some assume that the "expert" was language Professor James Liechti of Dalhousie University, Halifax, who was said to have made a similar interpretation.)

Edward R. Snow, in his book *True Tales of Buried Treasure*, relates that Reverend A. T. Kempton said that an Irish school teacher translated the stone as reading, "Forty feet below two million pounds are buried."[11] This translation has my vote, incidentally, as being correct. The traditional first word of the stone exceeds three letters and therefore is not the word "ten" but instead corresponds to the word "forty" feet below. A simple substitution-type cipher, when applied, certainly corresponds to the aforementioned translation – the code is broken no differently from the "crypto-quotes" one toys with in the daily newspaper.

By 1879, the bookbinding shop was under the new management of Edward Marshall and Herbert Creighton, as A. O. Creighton had either retired or passed away. Marshall's son, Harry, entered into the shop's employ in 1890. In a statement made to R. V. Harris and Frederick L. Blair in 1935, Harry mentions that he remembered seeing the stone as a boy and "until the business, was merged in 1919 in the present form of Phillips and Marshall."[12] He continues on to furnish this excellent description saying that:

> The stone was about 2 feet long, 15 inches wide and 10 inches thick [61 x 38 x 25 cm], and weighed about 175 pounds [79 kg]. It had two smooth surfaces, with rough sides and traces of cement attached to them. Tradition said that it had been part of two fireplaces. The corners were not squared but somewhat rounded. The block resembled

dark Swedish granite or fine-grained porphyry, very hard, and with an olive tinge, and did not resemble any local Nova Scotia stone.[13]

Notice also, that Harry says tradition has it that the stone had been a part of two fireplaces, not just one. This is not mentioned in some texts. If Harry and tradition are to be believed, Charles Driscoll's claim that McCully also affixed the stone into his fireplace has a ring of truth. Perhaps both McCully and John Smith enjoyed the company of that stone in their respective fireplaces at one time or another.

Harry Marshall goes on to elaborate that, apart from someone having etched the initials J. M. in one corner while in Creighton's possession, "there was no evidence of any inscription either cut or painted on the stone. It had completely faded out. We used the stone for a beating stone and weight."[14]

Finally, we are informed that when Philips and Marshall was closed in 1919, a Mr. Thomas Forhan asked for the stone. "When we left the premises in 1919, the stone was left behind, but Forhan does not seem to have taken it. Search at Forhan's business premises and residence two years ago [1933], disclosed no stone."[15]

In a last-ditch effort to locate the stone, thorough searches were made of the old bookbinding premises in 1935 as well as the Brookfield Construction Company (located at that time on Smith and Mitchell Streets, Halifax). Regrettably, the stone was not recovered, leaving us to wonder even now as to the whereabouts of this grand old relic.

Today, many challenge the authenticity of the stone and its glyphs. A skeptical view is understandable, considering that the stone has not only vanished, but also no rubbing of the stone's cryptic message is known to exist, just the replica commissioned by Darcy O'Connor. Some folks are suspicious too, that such a relatively simple type of code could have been used within a setting as apparently extravagant as the works of Oak Island.

The good news, however, is that hundreds of eye-witnesses are purported to have laid eyes on the stone along with its "rudely-cut" characters. Charles Driscoll in his book, *The Oak Island Treasure*, gives us a feel for the many people from all different walks of life who viewed that object when he says that "the stone was widely seen by many and shown to everyone who visited the island in those days." He added that, "Smith built this stone into his fireplace, with the strange characters outermost, so that visitors might see and admire it."[16] It appears that a good case for the stone and the traditional report of the existence of the glyphs may just merit a measure of respect. All things considered, the oral testimonies and first-hand sightings are considered good primary evidence.

Flooding

Relatively early in the more serious and advanced attempts at excavating the Money Pit, treasure-hunters encountered a series of setbacks caused by flooding. The incidents were so regular and disruptive to the project that they were determined to be intentional – that the pit was booby-trapped to prevent uncovering the prize believed to be below. A theory that there were tunnels connecting the pit to the cove has never been proven successfully. During 20th-century explorations, engineers and researchers tried using dyes to determine inflows and outflows, to no avail.

On this subject, Professor Richard Joltes has done extensive research. According to Dr. Joltes, Robert Dunfield, in the 1960s,

> rode the bucket of an excavator to the bottom of the Pit to examine it for evidence of the tunnels: he found none, and his dye tests indicated all but 15 gallons per minute [57 l] of the water was coming from below the 140-foot level [43 m]: [attributed to] natural infiltration from the underlying limestone bedrock.[17]

Tests performed by Woods Hole scientists in 1996, came to a similar conclusion. In one test, they introduced a sensitive dye into borehole 10X and monitored the coastal areas to see where it would come out. None did, despite the fact that the water level within rose and fell with the tide. Moreover, the water in borehole 10X was found to be brackish, indicating that fresh water was somehow mixing with sea water. The facts pointed to what appeared to be the existence of an underground freshwater "lens" on the island.[18]

Coconut Fibre

Sometime in the summer of 1850, members of the Truro Company were mystified about what they had unearthed below Smith's Cove. As they dug under the beach area in the cove, layer after layer of strange materials were struck, situated between the high and low tide marks, and said to stretch some 145 feet (44 m) along the seashore. According to traditional reports, no sooner had the diggers removed the sand and gravel beach surface, than they encountered a 2-inch (5 cm) bed of coconut fibre. Below this was found 4-5 inches (10-13 cm) of decayed eel grass, followed by a compact layer of beach stones – free of sand and gravel. The whole beach seemed artificial.

THIS ENVELOPE CONTAINS A SAMPLE OF THE
ANCIENT COCONUT FIBRE TAKEN FROM THE
TREASURE-PIT ON OAK ISLAND, NOVA SCOTIA.
ITS PRESENCE THERE WOULD SEEM TO INDICATE
A TROPICAL ORIGIN FOR THE TREASURE, WHICH
IN OUR MIND ALMOST CERTAINLY CAME FROM
SOMEWHERE AROUND THE CARIBBEAN.

Fig. 1.5 – Sample of coconut fibre taken from the Money Pit area. Courtesy Maritime Museum of the Atlantic M2004.50.91E.

Eyewitness reports state that great quantities of what appears to be coconut husk fibre was observed both within the Money Pit and in the vicinity of Smith's Cove opposite.

Another account of the fibre came from the late Mr. Hiram Walker, a ship carpenter, who once lived in Chester and who was also one of the early searchers (1805) on Oak Island. He related to his grand-daughter, Mrs. Cottnam Smith, that he had "seen bushels of coconut fibre brought up from the [Money] Pit."[19]

The Money Pit, as well as Smith's Cove, were locations reported to contain abundant quantities of coconut husk. Documentation confirms that coconut fibre found in the Money Pit and on Smith's Cove beach appeared to be the same material. After removing the sand and gravel covering the beach on Smith's Cove, the workmen came to a layer of brown fibrous plant and was described as such by McCully's crew (about 1850) thus: "the fibre very much resembling the husk of the coconut, and when compared with the plant that was bored out of the 'Money Pit,' no difference in the two could be detected."[20]

The nearest coconut tree to Nova Scotia is about 1,500 miles south (2,400 km), so it is not a stretch to recognize that its presence here was the result of human activity. Few disagree that the coconut fibre found on the island, and especially within the Money Pit, would have a provenance dating back to the original builders.

For many years, theories have come and gone as to the true purpose of the coconut fibre, or coir, as it is also called. Many have pointed to the fact that coconut fibre was used aboard vessels as common packing material, or "dunnage," as a way to protect cargo. It's no wonder that speculations arose that its presence in the Money Pit must have been to cradle and protect something of great value.

Cave-in Pit

The Cave-in Pit is located on the slope just above Smith's Cove on the island's east drumlin on lot 20. In 1878, when then-owner, Sophia Sellers, was leading her team of oxen over a spot about 350 feet (107 m) east of the Money Pit, the ground beneath the poor beasts gave way without warning and, according to R. R. Chappell, "they went down in a hole caused by the cave-in from six to eight feet (2 m) in diameter and from ten to fifteen feet in depth (3-4.5 m)."[21] Attempts were made to rescue the animals, and at least one of them was finally brought safely to the surface. The site became known thereafter as the Cave-in Pit.

The episode was all but forgotten until years later (1893) when Sellers related the story to Robert Creelman, a member of the then newly formed Oak Island Treasure Company. Led by Frederick L. Blair, it was one in the long line of gold-bug-bitten companies hell-bent to unearth the treasure.

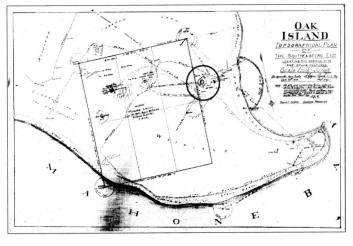

Fig. 1.6 – Cave-in Pit boldly circled. Oak Island-Topographical Map, 1934. S. Edgar March. MG 12.175 D.2A. Beaton Institute, Cape Breton University.

Fred Blair was particularly intrigued with the then modest-sized depression and had once confided to author R. V. Harris, in 1935, that "in his opinion, the 'Cave-in Pit' might be the key to the whole problem."[22] Blair had been looking for an air shaft which he was sure laid along the line of the supposed tunnel running from the Money Pit through to Smith's Cove. Experienced miners had once visited the island and informed Blair that for a tunnel of that length to exist (520 feet, 158 m), a ventilation shaft would have definitely been dug along the way. Of course, Blair thought the cave-in was the air shaft he had been searching for and that it was located along the line of the suspected flood tunnel. The thinking was that this might be the spot for a valve or shut-off to disrupt the flow of water to the Money Pit.

Excavation of the Cave-in Pit became the first order of business, and so the company undertook to probe deeper into its secrets. The cleanout started with the removal of some boulders and debris that Sellers used for backfill, down to a depth of around 15 to 18 feet (4.5-5 m). Beyond this was found to be a well-defined circular cavity 6 to 8 feet (2-3 m) in diameter and which appeared to be part of the original work. Plans of former Oak Island treasure companies were examined, and failed to show that they were responsible for that pit. This seemed to support the reports that the Cave-in Pit was indeed of the original workings.

Blair and his associates eagerly probed further into the pit, but then, around the 52-foot level (16 m), grave problems arose. Seawater began to enter the pit and the work all but ground to a halt. Eventually, it had to be abandoned altogether.

Interest in the Cave-in Pit flared once again when, in February 1966, Robert Dunfield attempted an excavation of the site. Dunfield had taken out a lease via M. R. Chappell of Sydney who held possession of most of the island. Some new light was shed as Dunfield reportedly found old timbers and two-inch planking and was able to verify an earlier account of fan-like drains located on the shore of Smith's Cove. But not unlike Blair before him, he found no evidence to support the assumption that this was an air shaft.

Chappell's Vault

A base of crude cement, thought by some to be a "chamber" of some sort, was found within the Money Pit by William Chappell. The records show that Chappell only discovered the vault when he drove a new test hole after the drill down a previous hole had deflected off an iron obstruction at 126 feet (38 m). His affidavit regarding drilling done in 1897, states that "A 1½-inch (3.8 cm) drill was put down past the obstruction and it went through the blue clay to 151 feet (46 m) and struck what appeared to be soft stone. Cuttings of this stone when compared, looked just like cement, and, as analytical chemists subsequently pronounced, samples from this material to have the composition of cement, it is hereafter referred to as cement."[23]

Chappell also hit what he thought was an iron plate both above and below the cement "vault" at depths of 126 feet (38 m) and 171 feet (52 m), respectively. Filings were taken up from the drill and examined with a magnet and said to be iron (then were unfortunately misplaced and lost).

Parchment

Nearly a century after the inscribed stone was discovered, mouths were again agape when, in 1897, a tiny scrap of sheep-skin parchment was recovered from among auger borings. The parchment, as mysterious as it is in and of itself, remains one of those tantalizing clues which grew to be an inexorable part of Oak Island lore. As expected, differing opinions and views have sparked various debates including the notion that the parchment was nothing more than a "plant," contrived to bait investors.

The story opens with William Chappell, who, along with Captain John Welling, was in charge of work on the island and one of the members of the newly restructured Oak Island Treasure Company in 1897. He had come from Tidnish, a little town just on the Nova Scotia side of the border with New Brunswick. William had been described by author R. V. Harris, as "a man of sterling qualities and character and a firm believer in the Oak Island story."[24]

It had been William who was in charge of the drill the day the scrap of parchment was recovered. Brother Renwick Chappell states that after William twisted and worked the auger on some substance struck under the oak wood at about 153 feet [47 m],

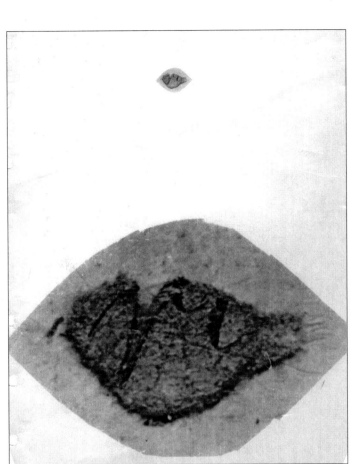

Fig. 1.7 – The controversial scrap of parchment (and an enlargement) recovered by William Chappell in 1897. Oak Island, 1969-1971. Photographer unknown. 81-571-5651. Beaton Institute, Cape Breton University.

it was carefully withdrawn and the borings brought up there with were preserved by Mr. Putnam. He cleaned the auger himself, taking all mud and dirt there-from. This dirt he panned out, gathering all cleanings including everything that floated on the water.[25]

Chappell later admitted that it was his experiences on Oak Island, from 1896-1899, along with his son's enthusiasm, that prompted him to make further effort. (William's son, Melbourne R. Chappell and nephew Claude, would one day share the same zeal and come to represent the second generation of Chappell's involved with Oak Island.)

Putnam left the island, taking the borings with him, and met W. H. MacDonald and Fred Blair in Truro, Nova Scotia. There, they examined the borings which consisted largely of wood chips, but among them was "noticed a few shreds of something of a different texture."[26]

Over the course of the next few days, during which time they never left Putnam's possession, the samples were taken to the courthouse in

Amherst for further examination. There, on September 6, 1897, and in front of a dozen or more men, Dr. A. E. Porter examined the borings. Looking on with a strong magnifying glass, Sherlock-Holmes style, Dr. Porter noticed a peculiar little compact ball, about the size of a grain of rice but with fuzz or short hair on its surface. Carefully and patiently, he worked the tiny compact ball until at last he got it flattened. It had every semblance of being parchment on which was written in either black ink or paint, characters that held the appearance of perhaps being the letters "ui," "vi" or "wi." The wee scrap was subsequently sent to Boston experts for further examination and was by them pronounced to be parchment upon which had been penned script, in India ink, with a quill pen.

∞

It is true that lack of evidence prevents us from positively knowing the contents of the entire document to which the scrap of parchment was presumably originally attached. For one thing, it is a mere fragment no bigger than a dime, the script on which doesn't even form one complete word. One former treasure hunter, Captain Henry L. Bowdoin, could hardly be blamed for his sour grapes reproach whereby he made the suggestion that the Money Pit had been "salted" with the parchment scrap. The insinuation was, of course, that Fred Blair and his crew had dishonestly planted evidence for the sake of luring investors.

Blair was quick to counter that the bit of parchment was first reported as such not by he or Mr. Putnam, but by Dr. A. E. Porter, who held no interest in Oak Island prior to his examination. (Dr. Porter's honesty seems to be reflected in the fact that only subsequent to his inspection did he purchase Oak Island treasure stock.) To use the words of R. V. Harris, "it was ridiculous for Captain Bowdoin to assume that Putnam used the parchment to induce himself to go bankrupt following a vain hunt for a treasure which he knew was not there."[27] Harris also raises some valid points speaking in favour of the parchment's integrity when he asks, "why not with gold and silver coin ... such a small piece of parchment would be the last thing to 'plant' in the Pit. Why not a piece of substantial size with history and figures on it?"[28]

Perhaps a closer look would reveal greater insights regarding this shred of evidence. For one thing, one could say that the medium upon which the letters were penned, that being proven to be vellum, does fit with the era suggested. The Money Pit parchment was determined to have been vellum, made from sheepskin. Vellum was an older form of writing media, made from the hide of animals, usually cow, but in earlier times in Nova Scotia known to be made of sheepskin. Likewise, the type of ink and writing implement also would be consistent with those used in the early 18th century.

Stone Triangle

The "stone triangle," as it is called by most, was an arrow-like arrangement of surface stones first discovered on the Southeast side of Oak Island by Captain John Welling, and subsequently pointed out to Fred Blair in 1897. The next time it came to anyone's attention was when treasure seeker, Gilbert Heddon, rediscovered the oddity around 1937. This triangle was located about 40 feet (12 m) from the beach and measured 10 feet (3 m) in length along each side with a medial line of beach stones forming an arrow. The apex of the triangle, if extended, would pass through the Money Pit located about 210 feet away (64 m).

Heart-shaped Stone

During the summer of 1967, Dan Blankenship, along with his then-partner, David Tobias, thought it might be prudent to expand their diggings beyond the Money Pit area and take a fresh look at the island's northeastern shore. In the thrust of his treasure-hunting exploits along Smith's Cove that year, Dan unearthed some pretty peculiar objects. From beneath the beach an old carpenter's square surfaced, along

Fig. 1.8 – A rare image of the "stone triangle" as it looked prior to its destruction in 1966. George Bates can be seen in the background conducting this survey (year unknown). Image captured from the video, *In Search Of: The Money Pit Mystery*, starring Leonard Nimoy, season 3, episode 64: frame 15:14.

Fig. 1.9 – Heart-shaped stone found at Smith's Cove in 1967, at a depth of 1 m (3 ft). It was found beneath stones suspected to be part of a man-made flooding system. The Smithsonian Institution confirms that the stone has been shaped by tools. Oak Island, 1969-1971. Photographer unknown. 81-561-5641. Beaton Institute, Cape Breton University.

with what appeared to be a pair of Spanish-style scissors and, oddest of all, a stone roughly in a heart shape.

The stone had obviously been wrought by human hands, fashioned out of a chunk of solid red granite. Its unusual shape led to all sorts of imaginings and speculations as to what the intended purpose of such an oddity may have been or represented. For example, the symbol of the heart in the Masonic sense held a particular meaning, so many theorists of the mystery envisioned some connection along those lines. The Knights Templar has been held up as being behind the mystery and the perpetrators, believed by many to have deposited something of a religious nature, such as the Holy Grail or the Ark of the Covenant.[29] Others have made the suggestion that it may have served as an ancient plumb-bob to aid in shaft construction. I wondered at one point if it may have been used as a small anchor.

U-shaped Structure

A portion of a wooden structure was first noted by former treasure hunter, Gilbert Hedden, in the fall of 1936. Hedden reported having discovered old timbers (15 inches, 38 cm, in diameter) buried under four feet (1.2 m) of sand, spaced 4 feet (1.2 m) apart and roughly parallel. The logs were also noted to have been notched about a quarter of the circumference every four feet (1.2 m). Each notch, in turn, was found to be inserted with a wooden dowel or pin. The fact that dowels were used as fasteners (as opposed to iron spikes) lends the impression that Hedden had stumbled

Fig. 1.10 – George Bates's chart of the structures (u-shaped structure) excavated behind the cofferdam at Smith's Cove. Summary of Work Performed At Smith's Cove, August 31- September 18, 1970. MG 12, 75 D3B. Beaton Institute, Cape Breton University.

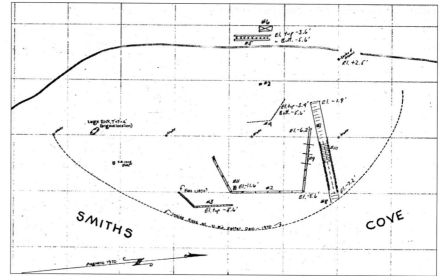

JOY A. STEELE

onto very old workings, possibly by the original builders. Sequential Roman numerals were found to be cut in beside each inclined timber.

But this would turn out to be only the tip of the iceberg so to speak. In 1970, Dan Blankenship, Triton Alliance Ltd., struck pay dirt in Smith's Cove yet again, unearthing what would, for me, turn out to be one of the most significant archaeological discoveries made on Oak Island to date. That detail much later.

Wooden Box/sled

Thirty years later, Triton Alliance Ltd. and Dan Blankenship exposed the extent of this elaborate u-shaped structure. After erecting an earthen and rock cofferdam around the cove's perimeter, Triton advanced inward to probe the area more thoroughly.

From about 3 feet (1 m) under the structure, Dan Blankenship pulled out a seemingly innocuous open wooden box (figure 1.13), measuring approximately 18 inches wide by 24 inches long (45 by 61 cm). The sides were 4 by 6-inch oak (10 by 15 cm), the bottom 2 inches (5 cm) thick oak, and the ends were 1-inch spruce (2.5 cm). There was also found what was perceived to be an oak dowel piercing one side of the box, which did not go all the way through, and therefore was not functioning as a fastener. The opposite side had a similar hole partially bored but was absent of the dowel-

Fig. 1.11 – Excavations inside the cofferdam exposed (lower centre) a u-shaped structure. Oak Island, 1970-1971. Photographer unknown. 81-576-5656. Beaton Institute, Cape Breton University.

Fig. 1.12 – Notched log found below original beach about 10 m (30 ft.) behind the cofferdam. This view shows Roman numeral IIII. Remains of a nail dug out of this cross piece were found to be of pre-1790 manufacture. Oak Island, 1969-1971. Photographer unknown. 81-563-5643. Beaton Institute, Cape Breton University.

Fig. 1.13 – Box "sled" uncovered from below the u-shaped structure by Dan Blankenship in 1970. Triton photo courtesy of Les MacPhie.

like piece of wood (perhaps rotted away with the passage of time). Also present on one end was a curious little square notch or hole.

As one part of the top end of the strange box was bevelled and jutted out to form a sloping edge, this artifact earned the name of the "wooden sled," and it was originally thought to perhaps function as a skip, to haul away loose sand or gravel spoil. But this odd relic lacked bottom skids and was also devoid of an anchor point or points for towing. In other words, the usage and function of the wooden box has never been passably explained. I go into more detail about this in Part Four.

∞

Many speculations have justifiably grown up around the true purpose of the u-shaped structure. One theory held by many researchers was that it may have been part of the cofferdam works of the presumed filtration feeder system (i.e., the drains). But the theory that the structure played a role in the drainage system seems to have been successfully debunked by authors Graham Harris and Les MacPhie (*Oak Island and its Lost Treasure*). To evaluate the assumption, the two examined the existing position of the u-shaped structure in relation to the layout of the drain system. They concluded that: "It is clearly evident that the log structure does not enclose the entire drain system."[30]

Megalithic Cross

Pretty much unnoticed until 1981, when surveyor, Fred Nolan, claims he first made the discovery, there exists a huge and mysterious outline of a Christian cross on the island. Nolan was once the owner of several lots on Oak Island and, being a professional surveyor, occasioned to probe and explore deeply into the island's secrets. For more than five decades, he did just that, investigating, surveying and keenly scrutinizing any-

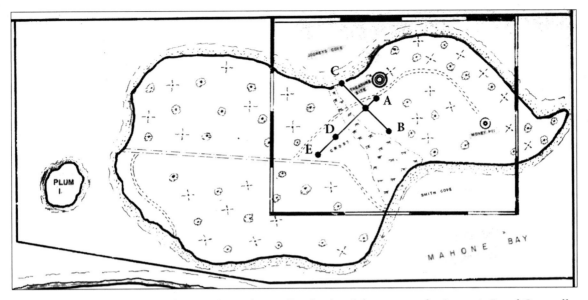

Fig. 1.14 – The "Christian cross" superimposed over the island and drawn to scale. Cones A, B and C as well as the "headstone" are located along Oak Island's east drumlin, while the remaining marker stones (D and E) are found on the island's western end. The cross structure, when viewed in whole appears to be oddly tilted, bearing between 55 and 60 degrees Northeast. Plot plan by Fred Nolan, courtesy of the author.

thing which may hold a clue. As in his professional practice, he would set about transposing his field data to paper so as to produce a plan of the site. It must have been both startling and exciting when there, on his plot plan, emerged the stunning image of a perfectly formed Christian cross. Clearly, the hand of man was at work, for this was not what one would expect to see in nature: the lines were too deliberate, the angles too crisp and perfect.

    Mr. Nolan said that a person could just as well be standing on top of one of those big rocks and not have known what it actually was. Nor would you know from just standing at ground level that you might be

Fig. 1.15 – Cone C is situated on the beach in Joudrey's Cove, Oak Island, and is one in a series of boulders which form the cross. Courtesy Petter Amundsen.

looking at but a wee part of a giant stone-studded crucifix. It sounds extraordinary, but this megalithic structure does assuredly exist; I too have beheld a couple of the huge stones which form a portion of the cross identified by Nolan. Just as the old surveyor had described, each boulder held in common that they were of similar size and shape

and also that each were oddly tapered on their topsides. Fred had aptly dubbed the mysteriously conical boulders "cones."

What makes the cross even more amazing is its shear size. The body, or stem of the cross, measures an incredible 867 feet (264 m) in length from top to bottom. Each arm sprawls out some 360 feet (110 m) across on either side.

Headstone

The mid-point of the cross, that being the intersection where the arms meet the stem, was predictably marked with a stone, but this one was different from the others. It rather resembled a human head, an eerie skull-like form. Nolan liked to call this median point, "the headstone" for obvious reasons.

Each of the other boulders, or "cones," measure 8 feet (2.4 m) in width at the base and stands approximately 9 feet tall (2.75 m). The weight of each cone is estimated to be in the vicinity of 10 tonnes. When asked how many other boulders of similar size and shape might be found on the island, Mr. Nolan reported that there were no others. He had apparently conducted a survey of the entire island, between the years 1961-1962, and stated that he had seen no other granite boulders of that size and configuration like those marking off the cross.

In 1992, ex-surveyor and engineer-come-author, William Crooker, went to Oak Island, at the behest of Mr. Nolan, to correlate the data and look over the facts first-hand. This was good foresight on Fred's part, for what better way to verify the findings than to have another professional back them up. And back them up he did, for upon completion of his survey he reported that, in his opinion, he was looking at a nearly perfectly proportioned cross that had been worked by the hand of man: "These almost numerically even ratios of body to arms and top to body suggested to me that this was no accident of nature; [this was man-made]."[31]

In a further statement substantiating Nolan's claims, Crooker declared that "the arms of the Cross were indeed at right angles to the stem, and all measurements complied with Nolan's plot plan!"[32] Additionally, he did as Mr. Nolan did; confirmed that the boulders were all of similar shape and size, and that there were no other boulders quite like these on the island. Crooker reckoned that the cone-shaped stones were specially hand-selected, probably from boulders on the shores.

It was also interesting to learn that Mr. Nolan claimed to have unearthed several strange objects around and under Cone B. For one thing, the remains of an old wrought-iron pot-bellied stove were recovered after the huge boulder was rolled over and its underside exposed. As they dug down and probed further, more fragments of the stove turned up along with, of all things, cutlery and shards of broken dishes. A number of small beach stones were also said to be unearthed (maybe used to lessen friction as the huge stones were being dragged into position).

Each of the conical rocks had to be surveyed into place. In other words, the final positioning of the boulders depended on where an ancient surveyor directed them to be placed so as to render the formation of the perfect cross. Mr. Nolan has been kind enough to confirm this fact.

When viewed in the whole, the cross appears to tilt at an odd angle, bearing between 55 and 60 degrees northeast. Why in the world would the megalith have been set up in that particular position? Why not set up the formation from north-to-south, or further away from the swamp? This was again brought up to Fred who agreed that there was "friendlier" terrain on the island where the cross could have been more easily set up and worked. There is more to this than meets the eye.

Other Things Worthy of Note

Tree Markings

Among the strange accounts produced by witnesses over the years, was one which reported strange figures and symbols scored on three oak trees then growing on Oak Island. According to a report published in the *Yarmouth Herald*, dated Thursday July 10, 1862, Daniel McGinnis had returned to the island to make a farm when he rediscovered the

> spot in question from its being sunken, and from the position of three oak trees which stood in a triangular form round the pit. The bark had letters cut into it with a knife on each tree facing the pit...."

Note that there were three oak trees (not just one as is commonly held), triangulated around the pit and all were marked with letters, or some combination of letters and figures.

Fig. 1.16 – "Letters and figures" carved into a broad arrow tree as was perhaps seen by the lads at discovery. [33]

Oak Cask

Jotham B. McCully of Truro was manager of the second treasure venture to set up on Oak Island. Operations got under way once again in 1849, with a return to the Money Pit site. The following is an excerpt, verbatim, of what McCully observed based on drilling reports and examination of the auger borings which came up from the Pit:

> In boring a second hole, the platform was struck as before at 98 feet [30 m]; passing through this, the auger fell about 18 inches [46 cm]

and came in contact with [as supposed] the side of a cask. The auger revolving close to the side of the cask gave a jerky and irregular motion. On withdrawing the auger several splinters of oak, such as might come from the side of an oak stave, and a small quantity of a brown fibrous substance, closely resembling the husk of a cocoanut [sic] were brought up.[34]

Stone Circle

Among other oddities turned up on lot 5, on the island's northwest side was discovered an enormous ring of stones that no one could explain. Paul Wroclawski thought the ring may have been 40 feet around (12 m), and he mentioned that the stones were very old looking (with that drab patina and moss that forms over objects left outside for years).

Charred Wood

An old piece of charred wood was reportly found while clearing rocks in Smith's Cove near where the box drains converged. In Renwick Chappell's document there is found a reference stating: "Work went on until half of the rocks had been removed where the clay banks at the sides showed a depth of five feet at which depth a partially burned piece of oak wood was found."[35] Burned wood or charcoal was recovered from multiple sites.

Fig. 1.17– Pine billet from "Money Pit" shaft on Oak Island, removed from the island in 1963. Courtesy Maritime Museum of the Atlantic, M88.36.1.

Pine Billet

The Money Pit was found to contain not only oak but pine as well. On a 2009 visit to the Maritime Museum of the Atlantic in Halifax, then curator, Dan Conlin, surprised me with the information that white pine had been recovered from the Money Pit. A billet log, measuring just under a half metre length, was shown to me; Robert Dunfield had retrieved it from the 135-foot (41 m) level in the Money Pit area in 1961 (see figure 1.17). Subsequent testing carried out by the Department of Forestry in Ottawa confirmed the specimen was indeed white pine.

∞

Habitation on Oak Island

There are inconsistencies with respect to habitation on Oak Island prior to 1795. R. V. Harris's research reports that the first survey was made in 1762, though no evidence is offered. Harris states, in a letter to a W. L. Johnson (June 30, 1966) that he had seen a survey made in 1785 showing lots laid off by Charles Morris, Surveyor General. Two more generations of Morrises were surveyors. Charles Morris (b. 1711 in Boston) "surveyed the whole of Nova Scotia in 1745-1746." Harris goes on to write that there were "no settlers on the Island in 1795...."[36]

We can see on the copy of a survey map (figure 1.18) by William Nelson (1785) that the island had been well-carved into lots, with owners of those lots listed as early as 1767. Researcher Paul Wroclawski, on the other hand, reports that the island was "divided" by Josiah Marshall on a plan submitted to authorities October 24, 1764. Wroclawski reports that the Poll Tax records of 1791 indicate that five men over the age of twenty-one listed Oak Island as their primary residence. Among early landowners were Anthony Vaughn (father of Anthony Vaughn Jr., "of supposed discovery").

Fig. 1.18 – Lot map of Oak Island, n.d. (origin in dispute). MG 12, 75. Beaton Institute, Cape Breton University.

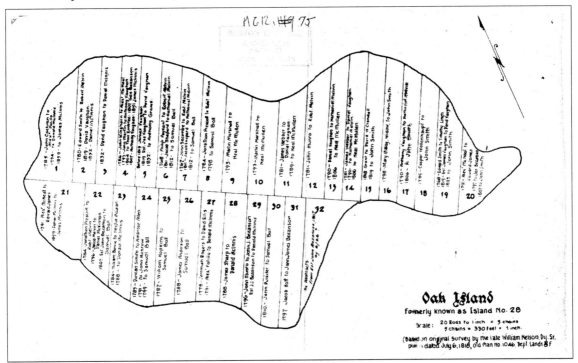

The Next Chapter

So, that's a quick tour of some of the elements of the Oak Island mystery. If one were to view the widely scattered artifacts of Oak Island collectively, there are tantalizing threads of commonality. Many more were carried away or destroyed during clumsy treasure hunts, but those above-surviving remnants – some questionable, some not – are clues that will come together as neatly as the pieces of a puzzle. By re-routing our thinking, effectively separating the wheat from the chaff, we can expose a new layer – this one of the truth. In what follows, I intend to give the reader a tour of a different sort: a thorough probing of the the island's history that allows us to go off the beaten path of the romantic and the misleading, opening the door instead with logic. This is my blending of historical facts and personal theories. It is my hope to explain more about the bizarre objects found on Oak Island and, ultimately, solve the mystery once and for all.

Fig. 1.19 – Oak Island Tour Map from a tourist pamphlet printed for Oak Island tours by Triton Alliance Ltd. Undated, courtesy of the author.

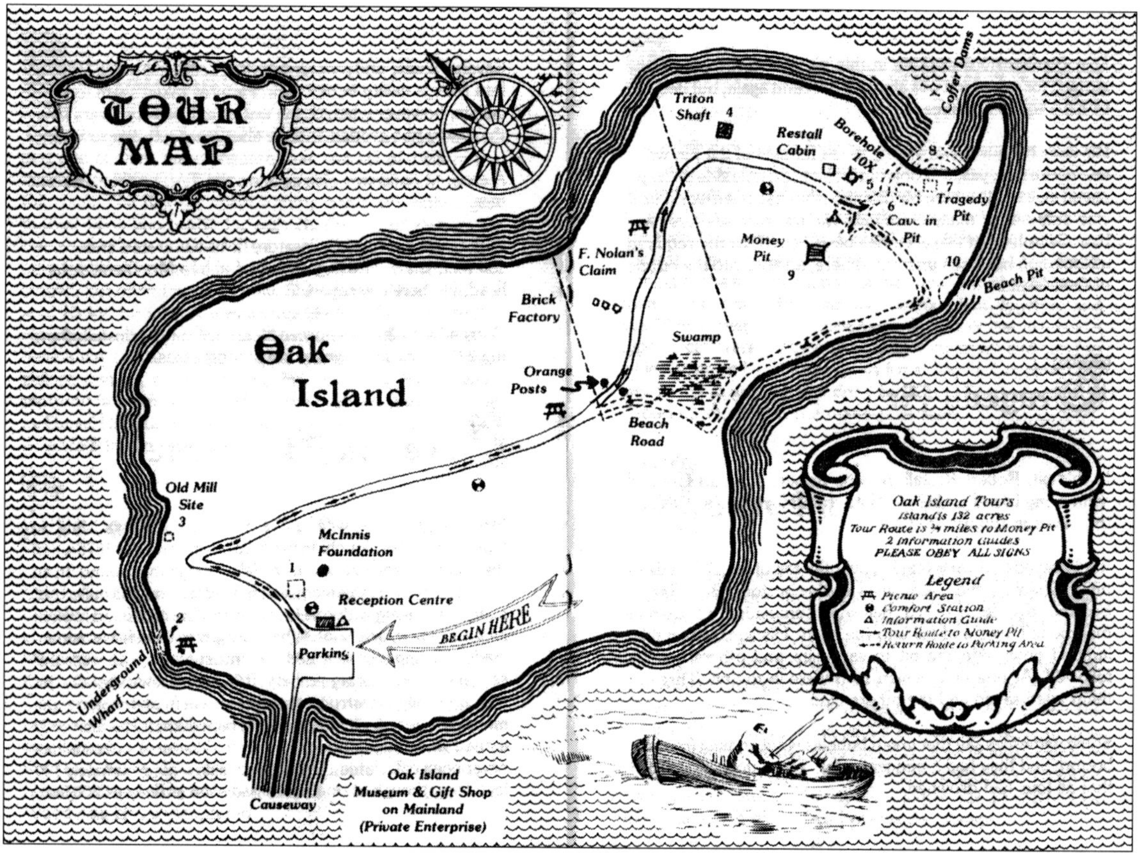

JOY A. STEELE

Part Two – Oak Island as a Global Enterprise

In vast Acadia's plains, new theme for fame,
Towns shall be built, sacred to Anna's name:
The silver fir and lofty pine shall rise
From Britain's own united colonies,
Which to the mast shall canvass-wings afford,
And pitch, to strengthen the unfaithful board;
Norway may then her naval stores withhold,
And proudly starve for want of British gold.

"Britain's Palladium" – by Joseph Brown[1]

You have probably not heard of this before. There is a little-known aspect of Nova Scotia history – world history for that matter – the truth and facts of which allow us to unlock a facet of a forgotten, even unknown, and fascinating history from a different angle. Oak Island was the site of naval stores installation, part of a mercantilist scheme engineered between the British Government and a company of English merchants in the early part of the 18th century.

Despite being a commodity of paramount importance to the ship-building industry of yesteryear, few people today know what naval stores are. In colonial times, the term broadly referred to and included all materials used in ship construction and maintenance – hemp, flax, masts, spars, planking, tar and pitch. By 1800, however, "naval stores" referred only to tar, raw turpentine and their derivatives, which included spirits of turpentine, pitch and rosin.[2] These derivatives, in turn, resulted from the "cooking down" of crude gum oleoresin[3] that comes from living pine trees, pine stumps and lightwood.[4]

For obvious reasons (masts, planking and pitch chief among them), naval stores became one of the most basic – yet most important – commodities sought by the Europeans in the New World. The practice of making tar, pitch, rosin and turpentine on the Atlantic coast began with the arrival of the first settlers. A report to Sir Walter Raleigh by Phillip Amadas and Arthur Barlow in 1584 made reference to "trees which could supply the English Navy with enough tar and pitch to make our Queen the ruler of the seas."[5] The report of a subsequent expedition once again made mention of "the trees that yielded pitch, tar, rosin and turpentine in great store."[6]

In 1608, eight Dutchmen were sent to Virginia to make pitch, tar, soap and rosin. By 1628, one of the early acts of the Pilgrim Fathers was to request that skilled tar-burners be sent to them from England. The Province of Massachusetts Bay (which, under a 1692 Crown charter, included Nova Scotia) endeavoured to produce tar and pitch right from their humble beginnings. Full-scale production, however, would not take off until the mid 18th century.

There is much evidence for a range of naval stores and related marine products having been manufactured at Oak Island, therefore it is important to offer more detail with regard to principal naval stores and their usage.

Naval Stores Evolve to the Colonies

England had manufactured its own naval stores since the Middle Ages, as it was able to furnish its own forestry supplies and materials. But as the country's navy and merchant fleet grew, the demand for timber and stores exceeded supply, and forests dwindled to the point of scarcity. Ships needing wood for planking, masts and fittings were in competition with domestic usage (heating fuel, building materials); likewise, industrial applications required fuel for the iron forges which burned wood charcoal. By the time the 17th century rolled around, forest resources in Great Britain had become all but exhausted, inevitably causing wood product prices to climb.

Having no alternative, Britain was forced to turn to European sources for tar, pitch, turpentine and masts. British shipyard managers initially sought materials from Prussia (an important exporter of naval stores at the time), but soon the switch was made to Swedish suppliers who were reputed to have produced the finest quality tar at reasonable prices. Sweden – whose domains in the late 17th century included not only present day Sweden, but also Finland, Estonia, Livonia and parts of northern Germany – had come to dominate the naval stores market and was established as the primary European supplier.

For the most part, England enjoyed a high-quality product at satisfactory prices throughout much of the 1600s. In fact, the exclusion of forest products enumerated in the *Navigation Act* (1660) seems to suggest "that England did not consider its dependence on Swedish naval stores a problem."[7] However, as the 17th century drew to a close, things were dramatically changing.

By 1690, a single firm by the name of the Stockholm Tar Company held the monopoly for the entire Swedish tar trade. The company possessed sufficient power at that point to fix costs at home and abroad and, as a result, prices began to soar, more than doubling in the space of just ten years.[8] It was a colonial-era energy crisis of sorts, and the English found themselves scrambling to find cheaper sources.

A glimmer of hope was held out for Russia with its rising naval stores production during the 1690s; unfortunately, their prices increased so as to capitalize on this high-demand product, effectively quashing that avenue. As far as mast naval stores went, interest in New England began to quicken around 1691, with the inception of a new charter being prepared following along with the reports and opinions of Edward Randolph.[9] At that time too, England was at war and, with that, there was increased demand for naval stores and timber.

Measures were soon called for to prevent New England from endangering a steady supply of quality masts to the Royal Navy. British authorities were aware by this time that masts from New England pine outlasted the firs of northern Europe by as much as twenty years (because of the extraordinary retention of its "juices"[10]). For this reason, as well as escalating prohibitions and difficulties in transporting masts from the Baltics, justifiable arguments were formed for safeguarding colonial forest trees suitable for His Majesty's fleets.

Realizing the growing importance of mast naval stores, a clause was inserted in the *Massachusetts Charter* (1691) requiring that "trees of specified dimensions be set aside for the use of the Crown." The *Charter* was the "first step in the evolution of a naval stores policy for New England."[11] The *Charter* took effect on May 14, 1692, giving birth to the Province of Massachusetts Bay, of which present day Nova Scotia was considered a part at that time.

With a mast preservation clause, the *Charter* had opened the door for naval stores on the continent. However, the selection of masts for his Majesty's ships was only one facet; much remained unsaid with regard to naval stores production. As a result, perhaps typical when politicians and entrepreneurs both smell profits, the subject of naval stores persisted another thirteen cumbersome years, mired in interdepartmental disputes and bickering.

Soon after the enactment of the *Charter*, government agents were dispatched to those forests claimed by the Crown to place a "royal mark" upon desirable timber, reserving it for Crown purposes. With axe in hand, pines for masts and oaks for ship timber were singled out and blazed with the mark of Admiralty property – the "broad arrow."

The broad arrow policy would one day spread to the forests of Nova Scotia on behalf of the British Crown. A thorough discussion of this little-known chapter of Nova Scotia history is long overdue, especially since more clues to the Oak Island story are contained therein. I will focus on this forgotten but fascinating part of Nova Scotia's distant past anon, and its direct connection with Oak Island, but for the time being, our discussion moves away from the supply of masts and focuses instead on those of the "gum" type, namely tar and pitch. I contend that these critical commodities are the basis of, and direct reason for, the very being of Oak Island's fame.

∞

The move to larger-scale production of naval stores in the colonies was motivated by government policy thoroughly imbued with the idea that production could be based there.

The Whigs, a reform party, gained political power in England in 1688, and they immediately came under pressure to increase production of naval stores. Their policies centred on what is termed as a mercantilist system emphasizing export of the "largest possible amount of products while importing as little as possible."[12] In 1696 the Whigs, through an Act of Parliament, created the Board of Trade[13] to regulate the empire's mercantilist structure. The Board soon determined that the system was not measuring up to its potential. In its opinion, not only was there a shortfall in supplying adequate raw materials for English manufactures, but they also thought that the northern-most colonies posed a threat to the British wool industry. The situation would be remedied, according to the Whigs, by shifting the nation's trade policy. Their theory was that English manufacturing should be strengthened, thereby increasing the volume of English shipments, while at the same time aiding the development of the outer regions of the empire. Naval stores production in the colonies therefore, would be the solution "to achieve all these ends."[14]

By the early 1700s, England's problems of securing Baltic naval stores, at reasonable prices, grew worse. During the Great Northern War (1700-1721), Russia overran Finland resulting in a decline in the latter's tar production. As if that wasn't enough, the War of the Spanish Succession (1701-1714) led to a massive build-up of naval stores that increased demand and sent prices soaring. At the same time, the so-called Stockholm monopoly further tightened its grip on the market by imposing limits on quantities and selling only through its factors abroad.[15] Moreover, naval stores commodities were forbidden to be delivered unless it was aboard the supplier's own ships. It was a double slap in the face that saw England not only squeezed to pay exorbitant prices but also interfered in valuable British shipping interests. The situation became chaotic.

Finding itself with no recourse, and a dangerously diminishing supply of naval stores, parliament was prodded into action.[16] As supplies dwindled to a trickle in late 1703, "the Board of Trade was once more ordered to consider whether pitch and tar could be brought from New England or other American Plantations."[17] In December 1704, dependence on foreign resources all but ground to a halt as the Privy Council called for a draft of a naval stores bill in the form of the *An Act for the Encouraging of Importation of Naval Stores* of 1705. Through this important legislation, England had come up with a brilliant incentive program that, despite its slow start, encouraged its North American colonies to increase their output of naval stores, while improving overall quality.

Encouragement took the form of premiums, or bounties, to be paid to producers to stimulate production. Additionally, these bounties served to compensate for high freight charges associated with transatlantic transport. The Board of Trade was "aware of the problems posed by

Commodity	Description	Bounty (£ Ster./ton)
Tar	Good & merchantable	4
Pitch	"	4
Rosin		3
Turpentine		3
Hemp	Water-rotted, bright & clean	6
Masts, yards,		1
Bowsprits		

Fig. 2.1

freight charges (three times as much from Boston as from Stockholm[18]) and by insurance during the War of the Spanish Succession (about sixteen guineas on a valuation of £100)."[19] Effective January 1, 1705, and authorized for nine years, the following bounties (figure 2.1) were to be paid from Naval funds through regular Navy Bills of exchange issued by the Navy Board.

The Admiralty was given the right of first refusal for up to twenty years of any colonial naval stores sent as part of the scheme. But at the same time, it was forced to purchase these plantation naval stores at inflated prices. The *Act* also made naval stores enumerated commodities, meaning colonists could export tar, pitch and turpentine only to British ports and only aboard British or British colonial ships. Likewise, the bounty could only be collected if the naval stores went aboard British vessels.

The second part of the *Act* was concerned with forest preservation, redefining property rights in the process. The Crown was given pre-eminent claims to all "Pitch, Pine, or Tar Trees," under 12 inches (30 cms) in diameter, three feet (1 m)from the ground, and growing on non-granted land, from Nova Scotia to New Jersey. Likewise, under this legislation offenders caught felling or destroying such trees would find themselves subjected to a hefty fine. No mention was made of mast trees because it was assumed that protection of them had already been provided for in the 1691 *Massachusetts Charter.*[20]

Colonial tar production was, for the most part, still in its infancy during the period 1706-1713. The Navy Board had concluded all but three contracts for New England, and those were for pitch and tar; there were none for turpentine. The value of those contracts were £768, £3,450 and £52. Of those three, it is known that there was at least one which was not fulfilled. Professor Joseph Malone describes in his book, *Pine Trees and Politics* (1919), that aside from the regular contract negotiations (of which no information was found), the "minutes of the Navy Board reveal thirty-seven 'tenders' of small amounts of colonial pitch, tar, and turpentine before 1711."[21] It would appear then, that no appreciable quantity of tar was being produced up to this point.

The end of the war brought with it an ease in labour shortages, which in turn set up the economy to expand and flourish. Things were definitely picking up in the colonies, as interest in the fur trade and fisheries were revived, and New England was in the midst of a golden age of shipbuilding. Without exception, each and every vessel constructed would require pitch and tar applications to make them seaworthy, and demand for these products began to escalate. With the ensuing peace, brought on by the Treaty of Utrecht (1713), came an environment in which the naval stores industry was finally set to thrive. Naval stores were increasingly woven into the local economic fabric, not only as a shipbuilding necessity, but also as an alternate source of employment to those soldiers now returning from the frontiers. In addition to England's seemingly insatiable appetite for naval stores, a larger growing domestic market now existed in colonial America.[22]

On January 29, 1717, England's Secretary of State, Paul Methuen, ordered the Board of Trade to provide an account of naval stores issuing from the colonies. Quantities produced there as well as recommendations for increasing production would have to be included in the report, which was to be presented to the king. A few months later, on March 18th, William Byrd was in England, proposing before the Board that naval stores production be tried in Virginia once more (despite a past failure).

Byrd informed the Board that America was capable of producing naval stores every bit as good as the Baltic, but encouragement would be needed. He suggested that by continuing the bounties for a further twenty years (with prompt remittance thereof) and making such stores duty free would serve to stimulate tar production.

Byrd also acknowledged the objections that arose in regard to plantation tar and the supposed damage it did to cordage. Cordage, or rope, was vital to mariners because it comprised the vessel's rigging. A coat of pine tar applied to the rigging was a necessity to protect it from the elements. But plantation tar had gained a bad reputation for "burning the cordage"[23] upon application, unlike the coveted Stockholm tar. To this, Byrd claimed that if the tar were to be made with the trunk portion of the pine, rather than from knots, and by following "the methods of Norway and Sweden, it will be good as any."[24]

All things considered, the Board's report back to Secretary Methuen resonated much of Byrd's belief in the high potential for larger-scale naval stores production in America. "We humbly take leave to represent some of the many great advantages which will accrue to this Kingdom from the establishment of trade for Naval Stores from your Majesty's Plantations," announced the Board.[25] The first advantage promised from colonial production of naval stores was that the competition with English woolen works would diminish. The fact that the northern colonies were manufacturing their own woolens was seen by the government as a great infringement on British trade. If the colonists could divert their interest toward the production of naval stores, it was explained, they would be inclined to purchase English woolens (rather than make them themselves), and larger profits could accrue to the motherland. Adding to this, the Board of Trade was quick to point out that the Northern Crowns would be prevented from monopolizing naval stores while, at the same time, freeing the kingdom from dependence on the Baltic supply which was "very precarious, and is attended with great expence in time of war."[26] The case was made and full-scale naval stores production should have blossomed at this point; but fate had other things in store for the northern colonies and their tar production.

England had made previous attempts to encourage its colonists to manufacture naval stores, but all had ended in failure. In the case of Virginia, the Jamestown colonists tried for a brief time to make tar. They soon discovered, however, that there was more money to be had by growing tobacco. In 1710, on the New York frontier, Palatine Germans also attempted to make tar. But these folks were unaccustomed to the industry and had no plans, proper instruction or preparations for production. On September 6, 1712, work was halted with the British cutting off any assistance to the poor Germans, leaving them to fend for themselves. They weren't long in abandoning the cumbersome and dirty work of tar burning, most turning instead to farming. It seemed there was always an alternative industry, yielding a greater profit, to distract the northern colonists from making the much-needed tar.

By 1720, the old English enthusiasm for the enterprise shifted to its fledgling colony northward, toward Nova Scotia, envisioned to be the next centre of colonial naval stores trade. The Board was adamant in its new focus, citing that past failures in Massachusetts and New Hampshire were because of "devious and scheming colonials." Nova Scotia, once seen as wasteland, was soon being touted as a "promised land." The Board reasoned that little success could be expected by trying to impress naval stores production upon a long-settled and mature economy that was established in other states. Therefore, pristine Nova Scotia – which had not yet been peopled by the English (it was, of course, populated by Mi'kmaq and Acadians) nor governed from Boston – was thought likely to succeed where New England efforts had failed.

On April 28 that same year, Colonel Richard Philips sailed into Annapolis Royal, Nova Scotia, to take charge as new Governor. He had with him "His Majesty's Instructions to His Governor in Virginia" that he might model this new settlement upon. The orders were clear; he was directed that all tracts of forest land, deemed suitable for masts and timber for the navy, should be set aside and surveyed as crown reserves. This was to be done before any other land for settlement could be laid out and measured. Also included in his instructions was an order to manufacture naval stores.[27]

Governor Phillips represented that the survey, to mark out the King's reserve of woods, was impeding the settlement of the country and, thus, the granting of lands. "When the surveyor comes," announced Phillips, "it will take two or three years before he can make any progress."[28] To further complicate the situation, unsettled land claims were dredged up relating to old patents and concessions from the regions first peoples, particularly in the region between New England and Nova Scotia.

Finally, in 1721, recognizing the delays and his incapacity to comply completely with his orders, Phillips made the suggestion that a royal timber reserve be made in every settlement of all woods fit for the use of the Royal Navy (rather than expect that every single pine stand in vast Nova Scotia be surveyed as directed). This, he reasoned, would "answer the ends of a survey and save time."[29]

As for his orders to commence production of naval stores, Phillips reported to the Board that he would "observe instructions to raise hemp and make tar, when the circumstances of the Province shall admit."[30] But that opportunity did not come, for the taming of the wild wilderness of Nova Scotia would prove none too easy. There was the domestic Acadian French population to contend with as well as their Mi'kmaw allies, who were much affronted by the encroachment of Englishmen on their territories. Phillips had his hands full.

Depleted by years of expensive warfare and left to bear the yoke of deep debt, England was feeling the financial pinch. The empire would be hard pressed to back any undertakings in the colonies given the war-depressed state of the treasury. However, if the nation could contract out the work, as we say today, and still maintain a British presence in the area along with other benefits which may accrue to the Kingdom, many of her headaches could be cured. As early as 1718, the Board of Trade had the king's ear informing him, "…if the Petrs. [petitioners] could be induced to settle in any part of Nova Scotia not already granted to any other persons, they might be made very useful to your Majesty."[31] Those petitioners were the well-connected principals of so-called charter companies.

The option to entrust the venture by means of government charter presented somewhat of a dilemma for the Board of Trade. On one hand, it could not afford to fund an expensive project of colonization, yet it was reluctant to recommend any more proprietary or charter companies. With this type of government-sponsored enterprise came a major disadvantage, that it vested people with tremendous power, which could lead to highly independent attitudes. Eventually, as shall be seen, the Board acquiesced to the charter option and made the fateful choice to outsource the naval stores program in Nova Scotia.

Just such a company, known as the South Sea Company, formed by a group of venture merchants, had been in existence in England since 1711. In a move that befuddles scholars to this day, these adventurous entrepreneurs were able to strike a major deal with the British Government, essentially swapping company shares for the nation's debt, which will be addressed more fully in Part Three of this book. Formed as a joint stock company, birth was given to numerous offshoot business ventures at home and abroad. One of those interests launched overseas, around 1720, was a naval stores enterprise located on a pretty island in Nova Scotia. We now know it better by its current name: Oak Island.

Naval Stores

Masts

Mast shipments, coming from the Baltic during the Anglo-Dutch wars, were often intercepted and confiscated, seriously curtailing the supply to English shipyards. To overcome this inconvenience, the Royal Navy turned to the Colonies and, by 1652, regular cargoes of masts again found their way to England, up until the start of the American Revolution (1775).

The earliest record of a mast taken from the New England coast likely found service on Henry Hudson's *Half Moon*, when, in 1609, he cut and stepped a foremast in Penobscot Bay, on the Gulf of Maine. Then, in 1634, the *Hercules*, out of Dover, loaded the first cargo of masts bound for England. Before long, English ships unloading at Massachusetts were cutting their return cargo from forests on the Maine coast.

The earliest account found of masts being taken in Nova Scotia appears to be in the year 1710, from Port Royal (present-day Annapolis Royal). Full-scale culling of suitable pines got under way after 1721; by the time of the French and Indian War, ca. 1754, these gentle beauties were already being depleted to the point of crisis.

The exploitation increased as the British demanded of Nova Scotia more masts than ever, especially given the volatile situation unfolding between New England and mother England. "By 1772, Nova Scotia was exporting to Britain about half as many masts annually as was Portsmouth, the traditional centre of the mast trade."[32]

If that wasn't enough, there were always woodsmen trying to eke out a living illicitly. Sawmills were springing up as fast as the trees were felled; everybody, it seemed, wanted their slice of the pine pie. As great stands of majestic pines fell, one by one, alas all that remained was the dismal sight of a clear-cut forest: a sea of greenery replaced by a gnarled wasteland of decaying stumps, scarring and pock-marking the landscape.

The Mark of Royal Property — The Broad Arrow

We were all of us young on the diggings in the days when the nation had birth,
Lighthearted and careless and happy the flower of all countries on earth,
But the creed of our rulers was narrow they ruled with a merciless hand,
For the mark of the cursed broad arrow was deep in the heart of the land.

"The Fight at Eureka Stockade" by Henry Lawson/Royston Nicholas

As the British brought Nova Scotia's forests more and more into the forefront of their naval stores scheme, a unique chapter of the province's history began to play out, escalating with the onset of Utrecht, the peace treaty of 1713. Cradled within this veiled yet colourful history of Nova Scotia's past can be found more of the clues to aid us in better understanding Oak Island's history. Perhaps author Winthrop Bell summed it up best when he wrote:

> To give an account of efforts at settling Nova Scotia in the first half of the eighteenth century without treating of this timberland policy, while it would not be comparable to Hamlet without the Dane, might fairly be compared with trying to present Othello minus the role of Iago.[33]

The broad arrow was the "British Government mark placed upon all solid materials used in ships or dockyards, to prevent embezzlement of royal stores."[34] Pretty much everything belonging to the English crown – from trees to canons – were branded.

The exact origins of the broad arrow policy is obscure. It has been recorded, however, that before 1628, a dealer in marine stores was prosecuted for having in his possession "certain stores bearing the broad arrow of his Majesty." When asked what he had to say about it, this gentleman, being very quick on his feet, came up with the reply that "it was very curious that the King and he should both have the same private mark on their property."[35] The man's wit landed him an acquittal of his crime, but no humour was felt by the English authorities who would inevitably crack down on this loophole. Woe to anyone after that who was found in possession of broad arrow property, for a hefty penalty was to be their reward.

The original broad arrow policy was actually the first attempt by colonial powers to implement forest management.[36] Essentially, the plan was to mark and set aside trees of suitable height and diameter for masts and spars for use of the Royal Navy. Government agents were set about in forests, blazing selected trees with three quick slashes, resembling an arrow, with an axe to the tree's trunk (see figure 2.2).

The Broad Arrow plan really appears to take hold in the colonies after the enactment of the 1691 *Charter*. Along with its mast preservation clause, the *Charter* not only marked a new beginning to naval stores policy, but it instituted a major change in the definition of Crown land. It reserved all trees, 24 inches in diameter (61 cm) or larger, growing on land not already granted to private persons, for use of the British navy.[37] This meant that ownership of pine trees of that size did not accompany title to the soil in any future grants in the new Massachusetts Bay colony. The penalty for offenders caught "felling, cutting, or destroying any such trees without the royal license," would be liable for the stiff fine of £100 per tree[38] – a considerable amount of money, given the era.

In order to ensure the proper execution of the above-mentioned instructions, suitable officers were recruited and commissioned by the British Government to oversee the care and guardianship of the forests. The overseer of this job bore the lengthy title of Surveyor General of His Majesty's Woods in America. The job description included not only knowledge of North America's forestry, but the candidate was required to possess a competent understanding of tar-making, as the process called for some fairly technical skills. Essentially, the Surveyor-General of 1705 was the policeman of the woods, a forest ranger and instructor combined.

Jonathan Bridger took up the work in New England at which he was known to have inaugurated the broad arrow policy with vigour.[39] In his letter to Governor and Council of New Hampshire, dated 1698, Bridger details his commission as follows:

> ...for ye supplying ye royal navy with what commodity I shall find here fitt for that service; in order to introduce a trade with his majesty's plantations in these parts, for ye following Specimens, namely, timber, plank, standards, knees, rafters, masts, pitch, tarr, rozin, hemp & c:[40]

Fig. 2.2 – Mark of the Broad Arrow. (Taken from *Yankee Loggers: A Recollection of Woodsmen Cooks, and River Drivers* – by Stewart H. Holbrook).

In 1711, further legislation called *The White Pine Act*, was enacted to prohibit unauthorized felling of "any white or other sort of pine trees fit for masts" not being the property of any private person nor measuring greater than 24 inches in diameter (61 cm). (The phrase "fit for masts" would eventually be dropped to avoid liberal interpretations by woodsmen).[41] By the time the Treaty of Utrecht was signed, the broad arrow practice was implicitly extended to, and included, the fledgling colony of Nova Scotia: "When the French ceded Nova Scotia to the British in 1713, the terms of the Massachusetts charter and subsequent parliamentary legislation were interpreted to include this newest colony."[42]

Hopes were especially high for Nova Scotia, for it was felt that, when ceded to Britain, it would become the centre of the mast trade. This is why, says J. Malone, the Board of Trade recommended that negotiators at Utrecht demand possession of Cape Breton Island (which was believed would prevent any French threat to the rest of Nova Scotia). Ultimately, Utrecht was decided contrary to British hopes, and Cape Breton ended up in French possession, at least temporarily.

As mentioned above, when Colonel Richard Philips sailed into Nova Scotia and replaced Francis Nicholson as governor, in 1720, his orders included naval stores production and procurement. To meet those ends he was told to "find by survey those tracts of land most proper for the production of masts and other timber for the Royal Navy lying close to the seacoast and navigable rivers."[43] Such tracts were to be reserved to the crown before any land grants could be handed out to private individuals. Instructions also said he was to strictly forbid the felling of trees saved for masts and hand out violations to offenders. Philips became far too busy with Acadians and Mi'kmaq to pay much attention, and, in his report back to London authorities, he indicated that Nova Scotia might not be any more suitable for a regulated mast trade than were Massachusetts or New Hampshire before that.

By the following year in 1721, however, it can be said with certainty that the King's agents were at work in the forests of then Nova Scotia emblazoning trees. (Present-day New Brunswick and Gaspé were also part of Nova Scotia, although Cape Breton was in French possession during this time.) Marking crown property with the broad arrow was actually "enforced" during that year and, as a result, extensive tracts of pine timber were reserved for the navy.

Use of the broad arrow essentially died out in the United States, with the onset of the American Revolution, but, as fate would have it, not before it actually helped fan the fires of that very war. In fact, the enforcement of this policy added to the already smouldering kettle of

Figure 2.3 – Pines of suitable size were emblazoned with a "broad arrow" to reserve them for the British Royal Navy. This imposition was among the grievances that led American colonists to revolt against Britain.[44] The Surveyor General of the Woods applying the mark of the broad arrow. From Manning, ii.[45]

colonist's resentment of English reign. After all, the Crown had essentially taken over an entire industry on which the colonies had been established for years and, you can bet, this only led to escalating and insurmountable friction between the two.

∞

The broad arrow policy opens the door to more clues found on Oak Island. As England's control of New England fizzled, Nova Scotia's growing importance was not lost on the government, managing to remain under the auspices of the Crown. The broad arrow policy continued actively beyond the Revolutionary War days. Records show the broad arrow being administered in and around Chester Township, at least until 1789. The following document (figure 2.4) can be found among the Nova Scotia archives, and offers a rare glimpse into the method used to mark out and reserve timber for the Crown in Chester Township (the same general area where Oak Island is located).

Oak Trees

Early French accounts make mention of an oak grove growing between present day La Have and Lunenburg. According to Joseph Robineau de Villebon, commandant in Acadia 1690-1700, "the soil is fair and there are a quantity of red oaks."[46] The oaks, it would appear, were native to parts of Nova Scotia.

Author R. V. Harris tells us that the original umbrella-like oaks, once found on Oak Island, "undoubtedly are red oaks, found along the same coast of mainland Nova Scotia."[47] Harris also lets us know that in 1931, one of these oaks was felled for critical examination after odd scars were discovered marking the tree's outer bark. When the tree was cut open, the end of a stout knife with a curved tip was found embedded deep inside. Running on the assumption that the knife broke off at the point of entry into the tree, the rings preceding the knife-point were counted, aging the tree from 1748 to earlier.

∞

JOY A. STEELE

With all the records considered, red oaks and white pines that once grew in and around Mahone Bay were probably among those the government ordered branded and set aside for the purpose of future naval use. Luckily, nobody came back to harvest the remainder and a few original reds on Oak Island were spared the axe.

One cannot help but envision the shoreline around the Mahone Bay of the past with its regal pines and umbrella-like oaks – that must have been quite a sight. The bay boasts a gorgeous seaside panorama, and few visitors would deny the unsurpassed beauty surrounding this little slice of heaven, even today. But imagine if you can, the Mahone Bay of 300 years past with its breathtaking seascape view enhanced, all the more, by a towering forest. To writer Henry David Thoreau, viewing the sun as it struck a stand of great white pines was "like looking into dreamland."[48]

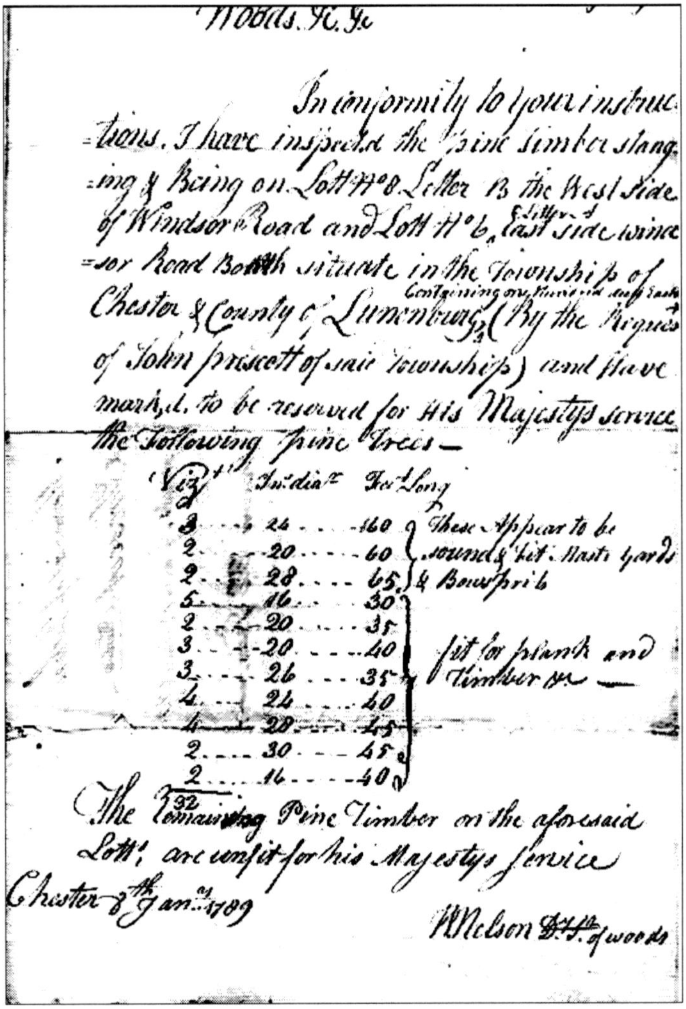
Woods &c. &c.

In conformity to your instruc-
-tions, I have inspected the Pine Timber stand-
-ing & Being on Lott No 8 Letter B the West Side
of Windsor Road and Lott No 6, Letter A East Side Wind-
-sor Road Both situate in the Township of
Chester & County of Lunenburg (By the Request
of John Prescott of said Townships) and have
mark'd to be reserved for His Majestys service
the Following Pine Trees —

Viz:	Inch diam.	Feet Long	
3	24	160	These Appear to be sound & fit: Masts yards & Bowsprits
2	20	60	
2	28	65	
5	16	30	fit for plank and timber &c
2	20	35	
3	20	40	
3	26	35	
4	24	40	
4	28	45	
2	30	45	
2	16	40	
32			

The remaining Pine Timber on the aforesaid
Lott: are unfit for his Majestys service
Chester 8th Jan. 1789

W Nelson D.S. of woods

Figure 2.4 – A rare glimpse at William Nelson's journal (Deputy Surveyor Gen. of the Woods 1789). On the timber tally above, Nelson states that he "mark'd to be reserved for his Majesty's service ... pine trees," indicating that he had branded and set aside selected trees with the mark of the broad arrow. Nelson is known to have surveyed lot 14 on Oak Island. Courtesy Nova Scotia Archives, N.S. House of Assembly Fonds, RG5 Series A vol. 2 no. 118 p. 2).

Ship Repair

Pitch

Until the application of copper-sheathing to boat bottoms was developed by the navy, after the American Revolution, pitch provided an effective sealant and barrier against the penetrating sea. As long as the era of oaken hulls and billowing canvas endured, this category of naval stores was critical.

Pitch was made by simply boiling pine tar (see below), usually in large kettles or sometimes in a type of ground kiln.[49] It took roughly two barrels of pine tar to reduce to one barrel of pitch. The end product is a rather viscous black sludge chiefly used to paint the sides and bottoms of wooden vessels.

An interesting account (1606) of the importance of early tar pitch-making in Nova Scotia was recorded by Marc Lescarbot, a French barrister, poet and historian. The story goes that a client by the name of Jean de Biencourt (Seigneur de Poutrincourt) invited Lescarbot to accompany him on an expedition to Acadia (Nova Scotia). Apparently, Lescarbot had grown tired of the practice of law, and Poutrincourt's tales of the Acadian wilderness presented an interesting opportunity. The invitation was accepted, and the stage was set for discovery and adventure in the New World.

Poutrincourt et al. set sail from La Rochelle, France, bound for the barren shores of Nova Scotia. In 1606, and after careful selection, Port Royal was founded. Poutrincourt was not only instrumental in colonization, but he was adept and able to ply his hand to many a task, including shipbuilding. As two of his vessels were nearing completion, Poutrincourt realized that he had nothing with which to caulk them, having inadvertently overlooked his cargo of pitch back in France. The concern and the importance of pitch can be felt as Lescarbot tells us: "But the carpentry work being finished, one only inconvenience might hinder us, that is, we had no pitch to caulk our vessels. This (which was the chiefest thing) was forgotten at our departure from La Rochelle."[50]

Poutrincourt knew that without pitch, his ship would be vulnerable to the attack *of teredo navalis* – ship worm – a feared and loathsome creature of the seas. But a tiny bivalve, this voracious pest was of considerable economic importance in the era of the wooden ship, albeit of adverse importance. Dubbed the "termites of the sea," they were to blame for many a galleon disappearing into the icy depths. This is especially true if the ship was sailing in the vicinity of the Caribbean, whose tepid waters teem with shipworms. Nova Scotia had an established trade with the West Indies throughout colonial times. These little pests were a great worry to all those engaged in marine interests.

The shipworm is not in fact a worm at all, but rather a specialized member of the clam family, notorious for boring into anything which is wooden and submerged in water, including the bottom of ships.[51] Although far less abundant in northern waters, shipworm was an ever-present threat, and local fishing interests appreciated the importance of pitch and tar as well. Additionally, other agents of deterioration had to be considered, such as barnacles and marine plants which, if not attended to, could impede a vessel's efficiency.

Turpentine

Another principal naval stores product, spirits of turpentine – may be defined as the substance distilled from gum resin secreted by conifers.

Figure 2.5 – A cauldron of pitch is heating up (right) in preparation to be brushed onto the boat's bottom. http://lesproduitsresineaux.free.fr/

Turpentine had relatively few uses in Colonial times, in fact it was not even regarded as a naval store until the early 19th century. It was, however, known to have been an ingredient in paint used to coat the sides of ships above the water line. Leather and cloth too, could be waterproofed with an application of turpentine. Some folks found it handy for medicinal purposes, including, variously, as a laxative, external rub and a flea repellent.

The "turpentining" process begins with the collection of resin from the living tree by means of a series of slashes or wounds inflicted to the tree's trunk (see figure 2.6).

Gum resin collected and barrelled is then carried to a still for further refining. The first generation of these stills were little more than crude cast-iron retorts, which gave a poor quality product. Apparently, a chemical reaction with the iron during the process led to the introduction of the more efficient copper-pot stills around 1834.

When heat was applied, a separation of the gum resin took place: the condensed vapours produced the spirits of turpentine, while the residue was rosin. Normally, only the highest grade or "virgin dip" rosin was spared, while the inferior product was allowed to run to waste by conducting it off via a wooden trough.

Rosin

As mentioned, rosin was the residue that remained in the still after the raw turpentine finished distilling. Rosin possessed few applications before 1800, although it was known to have been useful to mariners as a varnish and adhesive. Prior to the mid 1800s, rosin was not a commercially viable product and, for the most part, it did not pay to put it in barrels and send it to market. In fact, the barrels may have been worth more than the rosin.

Wood Tar

Tar could in turn be boiled down and made into pitch, but I am dealing with it last, so as to detail the industry of tar-making more extensively. Scientifically speaking, this method of tar-making comes primarily from wood and roots of pine through destructive distillation under pyrolysis; that is to say, a process of breaking down a material into organic compounds through application of heat in an oxygen-starved environment.

Wood tar is a dark, viscous substance produced by firing pine logs, stumps and other lightwood in slow-burning kilns. Tar was of vital importance to mariners because it kept rope and sail rigging from decaying. According to Margherita Desy, associate curator of the USS *Constitution* Museum in Boston, a coat of tar on the rigging not only waterproofed and protected it but made it stiff.

> This was important because the crew had to climb aloft. If the rigging was too flexible, they wouldn't be able to climb or they would climb more laboriously. But if you made sure your rigging was taut and then tarred it, it would stiffen the rigging and a sailor could climb it like a ladder. He literally could run up a tarred rigging."[52]

Wood tar was also put to practical use on land as axle grease, rust protective for canons and as wood preservative. Even livestock wounds could be treated with a coat of tar resulting in a lower rate of infection.

∞

It is not difficult to see how naval stores were of vital importance from the seaman's point of view. To the seafaring governments of colonial times, naval stores were tantamount to pure gold. Great Britain, in particular, has always prided itself on its fine navy and of how its ships helped found the nation. They knew too well that without a steady supply of naval stores, the Admiralty fleet was merely food for the shipworms. Furthermore, according to Joseph Malone, "at no time was this concern greater or more significant than during the wars for sea supremacy in the century before the French were driven out of North America."[53] Not until after the American Revolution was the demand for pitch and tar eased through developments in copper-sheathing methods, developed by the Royal Navy.

Considering the critical need for ship's stores, coupled with the fact that the colonies had an abundant supply of forest land (not to mention a growing slave workforce), one would expect that naval stores production would have flourished then and there. This was not immediately the case, however, and production on Oak Island did not begin until roughly

Fig. 2.6 – The turpenining process, beginning with the collection of pine resin in a turpentine orchard. Next, the resin is run through a still where it separates into spirits of turpentine and rosin dross. (*Harper's Weekly*, vol. 28, no. 1430 drawn by W. P. Snyder).

1720. Problems at home and abroad, dirty politicking and bureaucratic red tape frustrated British naval stores.

While still on the subject, in the remainder of this chapter on naval stores, I want to go into some detail on the making of tar; readers will be interested to learn of the many steps and components of its manufacture; the activity figures prominently in the history of Oak Island.

∞

Tar-making in the colonies hadn't flourished as hoped, until post-1708. A report by Jonathan Bridger, dated March 9, that year, tells us: "I last summer got the government to print directions and have been in most parts that make tarr in this Province, and have instructed and encouraged them to the making of Tarr...."[54]

His orders specifically stated that this tar was to be made "in the style of Finland" (referred to as "Stockholm tar," as earlier mentioned and as further detailed below), for the simple reason that it was superior tar especially for coating cordage. Conversely, tar not prepared exactly in this manner was considered inferior as it was said to "burn" the rope upon application (owing to its adverse effects on elasticity). Bridger's exact directions detailing the tar-making process as ordered by the Board of Trade can be seen in Appendix A, but I have surveyed a number of different sources and distilled the information below for the benefit of the reader.

These instructions, the very same on which the Oak Island works were modelled, were quite standard and ordered to be handed out to the governors of the colonies. The circular made it clear, in the very first sentence, that Nova Scotia was included in what they had to say. Dated August 26, 1719, the note states:

> Circular letter to Governors of Plantations on the Continent of America including Nova Scotia. [...]
>
> I am further commanded to send you a copy of an account of the method practiced in Muscovy, in making tar, which perhaps may be of use to the manufacturers of that commodity in your Government for the same reason. I like wise send you rules for raising of hemp. Signed, Wm. Popple."[55]

Tar Making in the "Baltic" or "Stockholm" Style[56]

Although many tattered descriptions exist which offer some detail of the tar making process, the following has been compiled to supply the reader the best complete method generally practised in the Scandinavian style – the method preferred by the British government. Emphasis must be impressed on this point because it bears an important link to the Oak Island story. The English were determined to have their plantation inhabitants manufacture tar in this particular style because they wanted to simulate/duplicate the well-respected "Stockholm tar"[57] within their own domains.

1. The kiln is to be built on a gentle slope, which sometimes forms one side of it (see also Appendix B: "Seven Common Elements of a Tar Kiln"). At the base of the kiln is the outlet, underneath which is a wooden pipe to channel the tar to a waiting barrel or hold. The kilns were most often dug in the shape of a funnel.

2. Gather stumps and big roots of dry dead pines. Referred to as light-wood in antiquity, this wood is rich in resin and plentiful in the 18th century.

3. The wood is to be dried, hewn and split into small sticks or billets, about the "size and thickness of a man's arm" (as one description read).

4. The roots of the pine, together with logs and billets of the same, are to be neatly trussed in a conical stack and let into the cavity (see figure 2.7 below).

The method of stacking is very important – all sticks must be pointed inward, toward the outlet at the pit's bottom. Tar has to ooze along these sticks down and in, to escape the zone of burning as quickly as possible (refer to figure 2.7).

5. The stack must be covered with a thick layer of turf to prevent the volatile parts from being dissipated. The turf layer is worked separately by two men, beaten down by heavy wooden mallets and rendered as firm as possible above the wood. Clay and mud can be used to seal the kiln and make it airtight. The stack of billets is then kindled, by way of insert-ing thin splinters of tar wood that have been set afire. No open flame is to be left, however, because the smouldering within the stack must go very slowly, as in the making of charcoal.

Turf functioned as an important packing material to ensure the kiln was air-tight. If a flame broke out and was left unattended, over time it would become very difficult to suppress, and the entire batch of tar might be jeopardized. A quantity of turf material was kept on hand at all times, because it would be in constant use while the kiln was afire.

In his book *Travels in Various Countries of Europe, Asia, and Africa: Scandinavia*, E. D. Clark portrays a nearly identical (to figure 2.8) wood-cut entitled "Representation of the Process of Making Tar, in the Forests of Sweden."

A. The conical aperture in the earth, to receive the timber; as appears in the middle of the image.

B. A rampart of timber is seen placed against the orifice from which the tar flows; behind which is a channel leading to the bottom of the conical aperture or furnace at lower left.

C. A vessel of cast-iron is placed at the bottom of the conical aperture or furnace which receives and carries off the tar as it falls; a figure of which is seen in the right foreground.

D. The timber is placed in the cone or furnace, left background, which is depicted with two figures tamping down the turf covering.

E. The instruments for beating and pressing the surface of the furnace when filled, appear right foreground.

A common feature of the Scandinavian kilns was that some had flat stones, or flagstones, placed atop the stack, prior to firing. Their function was quite practical, as they were used as what may be referred to as pounding or tamping stones. That is: flat stones provided a surface atop

Fig. 2.7 – Representation of "stacking" pine billets in a ground kiln. Tar being produced in a ground kiln. Illustration by the author.

JOY A. STEELE

Fig. 2.8 - "Tar Making in Bothnia," *Penny Press* magazine. Image depicts the tar-making process in action and provides valuable insight into the tools and construction method used.

the kiln on which the tar burners would pound with huge mallets in order to ensure a tight and compact seal.

6. The smouldering starts from the stack's surface and gradually spreads inside (referring back to the arrows in figure 2.7), causing the tar resin to melt, or sweat, out of the sticks. The tar oozes down into the outlet before it can burn or evaporate in the smouldering zone. As the tar exudes, it collects in a cast-iron pan at the bottom of the funnel, and runs out via a spout that projects through the side of the bank.

7. Often times a concrete basin was constructed to function as a hold for the pine tar that flowed from the slowly burning timbers.

8. Barrels are placed beneath the spout to collect the fluid as it comes away. As fast as the barrels are filled, they are bunged and made ready for transport.

9. Tar-making (called tar-burning back then) was not only very labour intensive but extremely time consuming. It took several days for a kiln to "run off" which, depending on the stack's size, might take from four to ten days, working around the clock. The bigger a stack, the more efficient the process and the higher the tar output.

Figure 2.9 is from a photo made in North Carolina in the 19th century and is believed by the author to sufficiently demonstrate the tar-making process as it was carried out on Oak Island. Notice the wooden barrels in the bottom foreground. The tar runs into a sort of cement vault, from which it is transferred into a collecting barrel that in turn runs into the waiting cask.

Naval Stores and the South Sea Company

One may now bridge the gaps and expand on more of the clues of this enterprise found on Oak Island. Why was Oak Island chosen? It is said that there are about as many islands in Mahone Bay as there are days in a year. Is it just a mere coincidence that Oak Island was selected out of 365 or so other islands?

In fact, Oak Island was specifically selected predicated on two main factors: land form and availability of specific trees. The island bore selection because it had a gently sloping landscape, lots of beautiful white pines and

Fig. 2.9 – "Sweating out tar from Pine Wood in the turf covered Tar Kiln, North Carolina." Underwood and Underwood, New York. Courtesy of the author.

good oak for shipbuilding. Moreover, it sported a central wind-lashed swamp, the perfect place to season and store masts prior to transport. Since it was also conveniently located on the seacoast, cargoes of raw naval stores could be easily shipped to England for refinement. Finally, as an island, it had not previously been inhabited and thus its resources were up for grabs. Simply put, Oak Island was the ideal location for naval stores production.

Much curiosity and speculation has naturally surrounded the identity of the person or persons who could have spearheaded an operation of any scale on Oak Island. Such an individual or individuals would have possessed political clout and sufficient powers to command a large investment and enterprise.

One of the links to Oak Island's distant past is preserved within the tattered pages of the Portland Manuscripts.[58] Contained therein is the following rarely sourced letter dated December 22, 1720, from parliamentary member, Thomas Harley, who is writing to his cousin, Lord Robert Harley (founder of the South Sea Company). The "island" referred to toward the close of the following excerpt is almost certainly Oak Island:

[Thomas Harley] to Lord Harley, at Wimpole.

London—The scheme for restoring credit has been opened in the House (as I formerly mentioned it) which met with little opposition, and yet the stock is lower than it was. The members are as docile as one would wish, but when stock comes to be put in the balance against specie, there is not enough of this commodity to carry on jobbing to the height it was in the late age of paper.[59]

The owners of stock and subscriptions complain but the annuitants cry out aloud.

Among the advantages to be given to the South Sea, they are to have Nova Scotia, from whence naval stores are to come. Mr. Secretary Craggs said in the House, if [John] Law had concluded his bargain with the Czar for all the produce of Muscovy, we must have been supplied from Arcadie.[60] They are likewise to have some pretty island in those parts, which is not yet peopled, and therefore more valuable, there being no one to hinder the planting right principles.[61]

The first part of the letter announces that the South Sea Company is to have claims to Nova Scotia to produce naval stores according to some near-future plan. And it refers to a stock option scheme I detail in Part Three.

The middle portion of the letter makes mention of Scottish-born John Law. Although clever and charming, Law had a dark side and has alternatively been described as a persuasive, gambling-addicted schemer who had been run out of England for killing a man in a duel. After fleeing England, Law slipped into Holland and eventually made his way to France, where he also put his talents to work. He managed to successfully pitch a debt conversion scheme to the Government of France, that captivated King Louis XV to the extent that Law was made his advisor. Among his schemes, and against British interests, Law also attempted to secure a monopoly of naval stores coming from the Baltic. Unfortunately for him, he managed to offend the Russian Czar in the process, thereby foiling his plans; thus the reference in Harley's letter. This brought about a counterproposal in London to give Nova Scotia to the South Sea Company, explains W. S. McNutt, who adds that "when a new source for timber and naval stores seemed urgent, Nova Scotia offered a reasonable alternative."[62]

But it is the last portion of the letter that is of particular interest to our story: Harley's mention of some mysterious "pretty island" in Nova Scotia is likely one and the same as our Oak Island. Let's take a look at that part of the letter again.

Notice the statement, "they [the South Sea Company] are likewise to have some pretty island in those parts" may be construed in the singular present possessive tense, indicating that the Company already holds, or has designs on, one particular island in some part of Nova Scotia.

Secondly, notice this letter even offers a brief description about the isle to which it refers saying that it was "not yet peopled" and "pretty." Common sense will tell you that the only way to give such a description of any place is for someone to have been there in person and actually seen that particular spot. Oak Island was not inhabited before 1720, and it still stands out as one of the prettiest islands in all of Mahone Bay, despite the ravages and scars left by treasure hunters and the production of naval stores.

For further evidence, refer to the list of ventures categorized as "Companies Trading to America" (figure 2.10). Among these ventures, was one proposal to import naval stores; more important was the fact that these naval stores were to come from Virginia and Nova Scotia. Notice the vast capital these businesses all held in common.

How can we be sure that the island referred to is one and the same as our Oak Island? Unarguably, there are numerous pretty islands dotting along Nova Scotia's coast and, back in 1720, Nova Scotia comprised much more territory then it does now. For a time she was called Acadia or Arcadia, whose territory excluded Cape Breton Island but included all of New Brunswick, Gaspé and part of present day State of Maine.

Furthermore, given that most of the South Sea Company records for 1720 have been destroyed or lost, is it possible to narrow our focus and reveal more precisely where in Nova Scotia, the South Sea Company had set up their island factory?

A. D. 1720.

America.
1, For settling the island of Santa Cruz in America.
2, — Ditto, for the islands of Blanco and Sal-Tortuga in Ditto.
3, Trade to the river Oronoko.
4, Ditto to Nova-Scotia, two millions.
5, Ditto to the Golden islands, Sir Robert Montgomery's.
6, Ditto for importing naval stores from Nova-Scotia and Virginia.

Fig. 2.10 – Partial list of the overseas companies trading to America.[63]

The answer is "yes." We know this because, fortunately, there is another set of petitioning documents including testament from a competitor seeking a grant for the same place as the South Sea Company. In other words, it turns out that the South Sea Company was not the only group interested in making naval stores in that particular stretch of real estate. Nova Scotia former governor, Samuel Vetch, and friends, had submitted their petition in London, on July 21, 1719, for a tract of land stretching out for several miles on either side of the LaHave River, a huge parcel of land by any measure (900,000 acres, 364,000 ha). Winthrop Bell, in *The Foreign Protestants*, lets us know that the "tract, as at first applied for, would have extended along the coast for several miles on either side of the LaHave River, running back several miles inland; but the exact outline of the proposal was altered a couple of times in the course of the negotiations." By January 3, 1721, satisfaction was still not forthcoming to Vetch and so "one finds this group intervening as objectors to a project that would have prejudiced their own proposal."[64]

A glance at the colonial records of January 3, 1721, gives us more information about the above mentioned "project" and identifies the South Sea Company as being the architects of that design. The Vetch group hoped to get a hearing on the issue for, as they saw it, the South Sea Company should not be granted any lands before them. After all, it was their group, and not the South Sea Company, who lent military service in the reduction of Port Royal against the French. Furthermore, it was felt that the South Sea Company was infringing on the territory they sought for themselves (to settle and make naval stores). Author G. Waller notes a remark later passed by Vetch on the issue, indicating he was afraid that any grant to the South Sea Company might include "the better part of the area they were interested in."[65]

We know, then, that the South Sea operation had to be somewhere within the vicinity of Vetch's concern. His petition reveals it was a tract that extended miles beyond the LaHave River, Nova Scotia. Oak Island is only some 12 miles (20 km) to the northeast and was, therefore, included in this extensive tract. The following excerpt is taken from the actual final (edited) petition of Samuel Vetch:

> Lords of Trade to Lords Justices [dated Sept. 4], Whitehall, for a tract extending from the harbour of Le Have, 6 leagues northward up into the country, 2 leagues Eastward of the said harbour of Lehave along the coast towards a place called Murlegash and 8 leagues Westward of the said River, with the Islands along the Continent, three leagues distant from the coast....[66]

The South Sea Company did launch an official petition of its own (but only after they had already been on Oak Island), reiterating the intention to produce naval stores in Nova Scotia among its primary objectives. At the same time, the South Sea Company also sought grants in the Caribbean (and other parts of America, not to mention a proposal to expand and enlarge the slave trade deep into Africa). The following will give the gist of the petition (with a focus on Nova Scotia), as presented by the South Sea Company in General Court assembled, to the King, dated January 3, 1721:

> Petitioners have for a long time intended to carry on considerable trade in America, [...] they hoped by your Majesty's most gracious favour, to have had [...] Nova Scotia [...] belonging to your Majesty, granted to them: – That by such a grant the said Corporation would be entitled to people, cultivate and improve the same, so as to bring in to this Kingdom Navall Stores, and other comoditys.... And Yor. Petitioners (as in duty bound) shall ever pray etc. By Order of a General Court, the 2nd January, 1720.[67]

In other words, the South Sea Company thought they had the grants of Nova Scotia, etc. already in hand. And take additional note that, like Vetch, they too mention their intent is to produce naval stores for the benefit of England. Further, it almost appears as if someone in authority had nudged them on for some reason. This confident notion of Nova Scotia being a "shoe-in," as far as the South Sea Company was concerned, can be found in another source and involves similar claims. This account was taken from an old book dating 1735 entitled, of all things, "A Survey of the Cities of London and Westminster and Borough of Southwark...." Among the pages of the publication lies a lengthy ramble about the South Sea Company. Not only is mention made of Nova Scotia, but it is purported to be one of the intended pillars of the company's stock, along with a part of Saint Christopher Island (now Saint Kitts) and their trade to Africa.

All evidence weighed, Oak Island strongly appears to be the island Thomas Harley talked about in his letter. We may safely state that Oak Island is one and the same with that which was being used by the South Sea Company as a base to manufacture naval stores in Nova Scotia, a little-known but very important and interesting piece of Nova Scotia history. In Part Three, I will describe another, less than savoury, chapter in the Oak Island story.

Part Three – Oak Island's Unsavoury Side

Slavery

The cornerstone of South Sea Company's monopoly was *asiento* – essentially, *asiento* is a contract granting the exclusive right to sell slaves in the Spanish-American colonies. A yearly quota was set for 4,800 people to be stolen and sold into slavery, which the Company endeavoured to fulfill with great verve (but did so only in one year).[1] Over the course of 96 voyages spanning a 25-year period, the South Sea Company purchased 34,000 slaves of whom an estimated 4,000 perished on the voyages across the Atlantic. (This translates to a mortality rate in excess of 11 per cent during transport.)[2]

∞

After being kidnapped and brutally tethered by the neck, Africans were forced to march – hundreds of miles in some cases – to one of the many forts or slaving stations located on the African coast. Dutch trader, Willem Bosman, wrote to a friend in Holland, in 1701, describing the gruelling process the newly acquired captives faced upon arrival to these jails. He writes that they are first put in prison altogether and

> when we treat concerning buying them, they are all brought out
> together in a large plain where, by our chirurgeons [surgeons], ...

JOY A. STEELE

they are thoroughly examined.... The invalids and the maimed being thrown out ... the remainder are numbered, and it is entered who delivered them. In the meanwhile, a burning iron with the arms or name of the companies, lyes in the fire; with which are marked on the breast....[3]

But the worst was yet come, for after being sold, came the dreaded trans-Atlantic voyage – known as the "middle passage."

By all accounts, the middle passage to the overseas colonies was sheer hell. Human beings shackled and stacked like cordwood filled the dank holds of South Sea ships. Disease and misery always accompanied these voyages, not surprising in view of the filth and inhuman conditions endured by the slaves. Those that succumbed to death aboard ship were promptly unshackled and cast into the sea without dignity or remorse. Sometimes the ill were callously tossed overboard – alive. Charles Johnson and Patricia Smith write:

> It was the nightmarish middle leg of a triad that had its beginning and end in England. From English ports, ships loaded with manufactured goods set off for Africa where the goods were traded for humans. The human cargo was transported to the Americas and traded for raw materials to be sold in England. It was a terse, efficient triangle, unaffected by the mournful wails of those forever lost. Or by the moans of the dying.[4]

It is difficult for many of us today to imagine such an enterprise carrying on, but it was legal, and carry on it did. Even years later, local newspapers would carry ads promoting slavery, such as this heartbreaking one: For sale "an excellent servant, 26 years old, with or without a child, six months old."[5]

∞

In 1714, seven South Sea Company ships transported more than 2,500 souls. This did not prove very profitable, not the least because the Spanish imposed heavy taxes upon the human cargo. Queen Anne moreover, held out her hand, declaring she had a right to one-quarter of revenue earned, without offering recompense for outfitting, rigging or repairs.[6]

The enterprise's trade in slavery peaked in 1725, but the Company received a crippling blow in 1750, when it lost *asiento* rights. The slave trade had been one of just a few of its enterprises in foreign trade. More on this in a moment.

If slave labour truly was part of the Oak Island story, it's fair conjecture to state that it was likely slaves who tended the tar kilns. Tar-making was not only smoky and dirty work, but it was dangerous. The use of forced labour in the manufacture of naval stores is well documented throughout United States history. After the ground kiln style of tar-making gave way to the newer method called "turpentining" (probably after new legislation in 1724),[7] slaves were exploited to tend the pine stands, or "turpentine orchards" as they came to be called. How many slaves were beaten, scalded and killed in the name of making of naval stores will never be known.

But it turns out that the South Sea Company was not acting alone in the slave trade, nor alone in the use of slaves in pursuit of profit. The revelation may shock you.

A Cruel Irony

The South Sea Company had an influential partner in this unsavoury business. A Church-backed society, whose mission it was to promote the Protestant faith to the four corners of the earth – and, of course, gather a host of souls along the way – was also engaged in a decidedly unholy enterprise. There were many such organizations of missionaries in existence over the centuries, but I want to address one in particular, that with the lengthy name of the Society for the Propagation of the Gospel in Foreign Lands – SPG for short.

Although not known to many in this day and age, SPG was a well-founded and abundantly funded society whose history spanned nearly 300 years. The SPG, also known as the "Venerable Society," was the missionary arm of the Church of England, the forerunner of the modern Episcopalian and Anglican denominations in North America.

SPG's roots can be traced back to the beginning of the 18th century, when London Bishop Henry Compton requested that Rev. Dr. Thomas Bray report on the state of the Church of England in the American colonies. Reverend Bray reported back that the Church in America lacked "spiritual vitality" and was "in a poor organizational condition."[8] This prompted King William III (King of Great Britain, France and Ireland), in 1701, to issue a charter establishing the society to provide the church's ministry to the colonists. After Queen Anne ascended to the throne in 1702, she followed suit and pledged to the Society: "I shall always be ready to do my part towards promoting and encouraging so good a work."[9] In keeping to her word she soon after, in 1703, expanded the SPG charter to include "evangelism of slaves and Native Americans."[10]

A pack of slave traders and a group of bible thumpers might seem unlikely bedfellows, but it is well-recorded that this is exactly how the two co-existed for a time. The South Sea Company used slaves, and the

SPG was always eager to seek out new converts. Wherever there were disembarked African slaves, the SPG was sure to have a presence.

By 1710, things took on a bizarre and disturbing twist when the SPG, and by extension the Church of England, became slave masters themselves. Planter Christopher Codrington had bequeathed to the Society his plantation in Barbados, where he was known to have kept several hundred slaves. Further evidence of the connection is found in Douglass (1755), stating that South Sea *asiento* agents were settled for some time at Barbados. Author Adam Hochschild (*Bury the Chains*) provides the following snapshot of the process slaves endured as they arrived at the plantation:

> At Codrington, as throughout the Caribbean, new slaves from Africa were first "seasoned" for three years, receiving extra food and light work assignments. Slaves were vulnerable during this early traumatic period when they were most likely to die of disease, to run away ... or to commit suicide.... If you survived those three years, you were regarded as ready for the hardest labour.[11]

Life as a slave at the SPG-owned Codrington Plantation was anything but pleasant, as can be evidenced by a high mortality rate among slaves: records reveal that as many as 40 per cent died within three years of arrival. Adding to their misery, new slaves entering the plantation had the word "SOCIETY" cruelly branded on their flesh with a red-hot iron. It was not their first brand, having been similarly disfigured by slave traders stationed in Africa, such as the Royal African Company, from which the South Sea Company occasioned to purchase their slaves. Prior to 1721, South Sea acquired slaves not only by their own ships but also by contract. Boys and girls, as young as ten could be part of the trade.[12]

Slavery was, in fact, practised much earlier in Nova Scotia than one might expect. According to the Royal Historical Society:

> The prevalent impression that they were first introduced into the province by the Loyalists has no foundation in fact. That any were brought to the earliest English capital, Annapolis, or to Canseau (Canso), a point of much importance, is uncertain, as no records kept by the earliest Episcopal chaplain at the former place are to be found: as to the presence of slaves at Halifax a year or two after its settlement there can be no question.[13]

It is known that slaves were a part of everyday living among elites in Louisbourg during its 40-plus-year history (1713-1758). Both SPG and the South Sea Company were operating in Nova Scotia in the early 1720s. Annapolis Royal Governor Richard Phillips's council for public affairs included Rev. John Harrison, SPG, chaplain to the 40th regiment.

Evidence has also been uncovered – not surprising in view of this bizarre association between clergy and slavers – that the church held shares in the South Sea Company. At Lambeth Palace Library in London there is housed an excellent collection of SPG history. Resting among the records can be found a warrant by Archbishop William Wake for the sale of South Sea stock, dated May 6, 1721. Similar warrants ranging in years from 1722-1732 point to several bishops who bought slaver stock, including the Bishops of Norwich (John Leng), Rochester (Samuel Bradford), St. Asaph (Thomas Tanner), St. David's (Adam Ottley) and Durham (William Talbot). Apparently, these good clergy never saw the sin in human trafficking.

In 2006, the General Synod of the Church of England formally apologized for their direct role in the slave trade. Reverend Simon Bessant was quoted as saying, "We were directly responsible for what happened. In the sense of inheriting our history, we can say we owned slaves, we branded slaves, that is why I believe we must actually recognise our history and offer an apology."[14]

Reverend Bessant also pointed out that when emancipation of slaves came about in 1833, compensation was paid to the owners and not to the slaves. He cited one case in which the Bishop of Exeter and three colleagues were paid almost £13,000 as compensation for having to free 665 slaves.

Fig. 3.1 – This medallion was struck, in 1976, in commemoration of the 1870 formation of the Colored Methodist Episcopal Church (name changed to Christian Methodist Episcopal Church (CME) in 1952). On the reverse is included "an authentic copy of a pass to freedom."

∞

The Virginia manifesto (the guide for settlement handed to Col. Richard Phillips) states it clearly: colonize and fortify the frontiers, make naval stores and spread the Protestant religion. Governor Alexander Spotswood was following the same guide and doing the same things in

Virginia by 1720. He encouraged settlement, strengthened and expanded the frontiers, made tar and built Fort Christanna – a school to religiously convert and teach indigenous people. The superpowers of yesteryear were not only in conflict over territory but very much engaged in an all-out religious offensive. As Carl Bridenbaugh so aptly put it about the SPG, it was "British imperialism in ecclesiastical guise."[15]

The mutual relationship of the two corporations also afforded a measure of protection to the lay missionaries, who otherwise might have faced grave dangers in the wild and unsettled land. The SPG, in addition to church business, was known to be enterprising both directly and indirectly in their mingling with the slavers. Their charter shows that the Society held as one of their primary objectives to provide "maintenance for an orthodox clergy in the plantations, colonies, and factories of Great Britain beyond the seas, for the instruction of the King's loving subjects in the Christian religion."[16]

It wasn't always a "match made in heaven" between the slavers and the SPG, for the slave masters were at first recalcitrant toward a church presence around the slaves – caring neither for saving souls, nor for education. As well, conversion of the slaves, who were considered less-than-human, to Christianity risked them being so regarded, as people with rights.

George Whitfield, an English Anglican preacher, probably best summed up the ill treatment of slaves in a 1740 open letter to the inhabitants of Maryland, Virginia and North and South Carolina. The letter castigates slave masters "for working their slaves as if they were dogs, for punishing them barbarously, and for failing to Christianize them."[17]

To convince the slave masters that their holy presence was of importance, the SPG argued that a baptized slave population would become all the more docile, obedient and thus more easily controllable. Their logic suited the partners just fine. The SPG could win souls, and the slaver could assert almost uncontested control. Their mutual collaboration was likewise smiled on by the Crown, who held to the agenda of proselytization in Nova Scotia. No doubt, slave labour was employed in the manufacture of naval stores on Oak Island.

My thoughts return to that gruesome visual that Dan Blankeship recounted – a severed hand in the depths of borehole 10X. Could it be that Oak Island once also harboured a slave keep or dungeon designed to imprison people? It might also account for the discovery of a large I-beam and crossbeams and the pieces of the dated chain. It is true that the hand was cleanly severed, almost as if snapped from a wrist manacle – maybe as the drill passed through. And if that is true, the dastardly implication is that this person or persons met their demise while still chained and helpless. It melts one's heart to think of it.

The Bubble Bursts

I can calculate the movement of the stars, but not the madness of men.

Sir Isaac Newton on the South Sea Bubble.[18]

Slavery; South Sea Company; SPG: What do all these things have to do with the Oak Island mystery? The answer lies tangled up in one of the biggest financial disasters in history: The South Sea Bubble. It was an economic disaster of epic proportion brought on mainly by speculation of company stock. When the bubble burst in 1720, the aftermath brought with it waves of panic, coupled with the sting of financial ruin, to many ill-fated investors throughout the British Empire and beyond. Oak Island, and the naval stores produced there, was but one casualty among many ruined and abandoned enterprises.

∞

Responsibility for all of this was none other than the South Sea Company, earlier described. The origin of the South Sea Company may be traced to Robert Harley (later Earl of Oxford). In August 1710, almost as soon as Harley took office as Chancellor of the Exchequer, he was confronted with the unwieldy task of improving England's finances. The government was eager to take measures to discharge the national debt which, by this time, amounted to in excess of £9 million, an enormous sum of money, given the era.

The following year, Harley and others, including John Blunt (previous director of the Sword Blade Company), established the Governor and Company of Merchants of Great Britain Trading to the South Seas and Other Parts of America – the South Sea Company, as it came to be known. The South Sea Company began in earnest as a joint stock company granted by the English Government sole trade to the Spanish West Indies, exclusive of all other nations except, of course, Spain. The deal made provision of a guaranteed annual interest payment to the company of 6 per cent. In exchange, the South Sea Company agreed to take over and consolidate the national debt, mainly incurred during years of warfare, especially due to its long conflict with Spain. The plan was to be executed by swapping South Sea Company stock for the nation's debt which parliament eagerly embraced. It must be mentioned, however, that expectations were running prematurely high as these trading rights were presupposed depending on the successful conclusion of the War of the Spanish Succession.

That War was effectively ended with the Treaty of Utrecht in 1713, but the glad tidings on which one Robert Harley had pinned his hopes instead delivered unhappy shortcomings. The actual rights granted in the treaty were not nearly as wide-ranging as Harley had originally anticipated. For one thing, the company was only permitted to send one trading ship of goods per year to the Spanish colonies; a far cry from its expectations for trading riches. Trading stations were, however, permitted to be set up at seven locations in Spanish America including Cartagena, Vera Cruz, Buenos Aires, Havana, Caracas, Panama and Portobello.[19]

In 1718 things pretty much went from mediocre to bad for the South Sea Company due to another breakout of war with Spain. Furthermore, England was faring no better off as the national debt continued to mount. By 1719, the London newspaper, *Weekly Journal*, reported in its December 5 issue that "many thousands of our manufacturers are now out of work," and added that "one half of those at present employed are kept at work only upon the hope of some relief from this session of Parliament."[20] Without a doubt, something had to be done, and John Blunt saw just the opening he needed to promote a bailout scheme concocted in late 1719. South Sea directors proposed that an *Act* of Parliament convert successive portions of the national debt into South Sea shares. Parliament took the bait and approved the proposal resulting in another fresh issue of South Sea stock.

It was around this time too, that King Phillip of Spain had a surprising change of heart and declared he would like to strike a peace deal with England. Hopes were sparked anew as the prospects for trade to Spanish America once more became a realistic possibility. Unfortunately, however, this was only to be the calm proceeding a massive financial storm about to sweep the nation, a storm that crossed the ocean.

South Sea shares were trading at a modest £128 by January 1720, and so the Company undertook "measures" to stimulate interest. Bribes were handed out to several members of parliament; insider-trading to pump up the shares ensued, and false and misleading statements were passed around in the House. Following this came a propaganda campaign aimed at the public in hopes of stirring up greater interest in the company's stock. Rumours of South Sea riches and bogus claims of success were circulated by the directors. Visions of opulence and wealth seized the imaginations of the general public and merchants alike. Big-name officials, and other people of repute, were solicited to act as front men.

Even King George I, unwittingly, allowed the Company to suck him into the scheme.

Interest was furthered when the government backed another proposal from the company by which it would assume yet more of the nation's debt, again by exchanging new shares of company stock. The South Sea Company's bid was even more preferential than that of its chief competitor (the Bank of England); on April 7, 1720, the House of Lords approved the plan.

Meanwhile, the company's publicity tactics had evidently worked, for the public was by this time whipped into a frenzy, attempting to get their hands on South Sea stock. On April 14, £2 million of South Sea stock was offered to the public at £300 per share, of which only 20 per cent had to be paid in advance. A million pounds sterling was snapped up within an hour of opening.[21]

No longer was luxury reserved for the aristocracy, nor was gender an issue when it came to investing in the stock market. Men and women of all classes were welcome to partake of the gamble – before long, many a patron willingly traded their nesteggs just for a chunk of South Sea stock. The nation became enraptured with the company and what trading ventures lay in store in the New World. People reminisced about the exploits of Drake and revived the dreams of Raleigh. "This spirit spread through the whole nation, and many, who America scarcely knew the whereabouts lies, felt nonetheless quite certain of its being strewed with gold and gems."[22]

Fig. 3.2 – The public was obsessed with stock-jobbing which ran rife during the bubble crisis of 1720. (From *Cassell's Illustrated History of England*, ca. 1860, courtesy of author).

The stock had begun its meteoric rise and, as a result of this apparent success, a host of many imitator joint stock companies began to appear and jostle for a share of the lucrative market. "Bubble companies," as they came to be known, literally popped up overnight to cash in on the speculative mania, which by this time had completely gripped the nation. Some of these ventures appeared posed to operate on a sound basis, but most were wildcat schemes launched to dupe the gullible. Still, investors were so

JOY A. STEELE

keen to buy rising stocks that even the most outrageous in design had people queuing up in droves.

Among some of the companies, or "bubbles," which morphed into existence, was one for the transmutation of quicksilver into malleable fine metal. Another claimed it could form sawdust into usable boards, free of knots. My favourite: "for carrying on an undertaking of great advantage, but nobody to know what it is."[23] By the time the broker closed up shop at 3 p.m., he found that he had accumulated a whopping £2,000. That very same evening he skipped off to Europe, along with the investors' loot, never to be heard from again.

The intensity of speculation taking place during the summer of 1720, subjected public credit to great strain. In an effort to divert capital away from competition arising from the other bubble companies, the South Sea directors appealed to the government to intervene. This turned out to be the most fateful decision that the directors would ever make, for it sparked a chain of events leading to the company's near ruin and plunged the British empire into pandemonium.

Presumably at the instigation of the South Sea Company, Parliament passed a bill named the *Royal Exchange and London Assurance Corporation Act 1719*, known to history as the *Bubble Act*, on June 9, 1720. The *Act* prohibited establishment of any company without a Royal Charter and, likewise, collapsed those companies of lesser note which were speculative in nature. Seemingly overnight, a host of bubble companies dropped like flies.

More prosecutions were carried out by the government and subsequently, published in the London *Gazette* of August 20, announcing that they had given express directions to bring writs (called Scire Facias[24]) against the charters or patents of the following "pretended companies promulgated contrary to law"[25]: York Buildings Company, Lustring Company, English Copper and Welsh Copper and Lead.

The public, seeing the mayhem, had no way of knowing to what extent the proceedings might degenerate, and so they began to withdraw their money from their speculations. This, of course, adversely impacted South Sea stock which began to rapidly tumble downward. In the space of just one month – August 20 to September 19, 1720 – the stock price crashed to £450 (its highest point was around £1,000 near the end of June). As September was drawing to a close, the panic reached its worst – stock prices continued to plummet.

The great economic bubble finally burst, spewing forth the fury of hell upon the English economy. One newsletter circulated in 1721 sums up the aftermath in England – quoting Daniel Defoe – saying:

Here appears the cause of widows' sighs, the orphans' tears, the ruin of families, the distress of millions, the sinking of credit, the discouragement of trade, the lowering of our stocks. Here we see who have been lavish of the nation's wealth, and squandered away our treasure to help undo us....[26]

It is said that complete and utter chaos crossed the land, as folks struggled to absorb the shocking reality that they had just lost everything – not to mention that the whole country was broke. Parliament too, was in an uproar and, predictably, finger-pointing ensued. An all-out witch hunt was soon launched against the directors of the South Sea Company, who by this time, had become quite demonized by all of England. The *Penny Magazine* August 6, 1842, issue is quoted as saying: "A director was scarcely safe in the streets from the vengeance of the populace...." One member of the House, a Mr. Molesworth, was particularly vehement toward the errant directors as he huffed out what he thought ought to be fitting punishment: "Follow the example of the ancient Romans," he began, "they adjudged the guilty wretch to be sown in a sack, and thrown alive into the Tyber ... and [I] should be satisfied to see them tied, in like manner in sacks, and thrown into the Thames!"[27]

Having a valid charter and what appears to be solid backing and even urging by authorities, the South Sea Company would have had little reason not to continue to work, or to concentrate, on Oak Island. Indeed, referring again to Thomas Harley's letter to his cousin Lord Robert Harley (see page 71), dated December 22, 1720, it appears that "the scheme for restoring credit" almost certainly includes a continuation of naval stores production on the island.[28] There is no doubt that the company was in trouble as a result of the bubble, but I would suggest that the Oak Island operation, at whatever stage it was at the time, was anticipated to be one of the company's saving graces.

As further evidence, almost as if referring directly to Oak Island, it is recorded that, after the speculative bubble burst, Samuel Vetch "hurriedly

Fig. 3.3 – The South Sea Bubble. Thousands were ruined, but stockbrokers (and pawnbrokers) had a good year. Illustration from *Beagle Archive*.

pledged that any lands his group received would not become the object of speculation."[29] This seemingly defensive move might also indicate that South Sea Company was already working in the area.

Further, the South Sea Company petitioned the Crown in January of 1721, stating that

> the petitioners [South Sea Company] intended to carry on a considerable Trade ... especially on the passing [of] the last Act of Parliament for taking in public [monies], when they hoped ... to have had ... Nova Scotia....

> [And] that by such a grant, the said Corporation would be entitled to People, cultivate and Improve ... or as to bring into this Kingdom Navall Stores, and other [commodities], now brought in from Foreign Parts.[30]

> The company ... in their distress petitioned the king for a grant ... for the country of Nova Scotia, for the advantage of their trade.[31]

∞

Although we cannot be precise about when South Sea Company's naval stores operations on Oak Island began, the evidence suggests that, at the very least, the summer of 1720 saw lots of activity. We can, however, come close to knowing when it ended. As part of what today might be termed a "bail-out," South Sea was:

> granted with a proviso that from Midsummer 1722, two millions of the company's capital stock should be annihilated for the benefit of the public....[32]

As South Sea shares sank into oblivion, so too did the little Oak Island factory slip away with the wreckage. Exactly when she fell cannot be stated with certainty, though the official demise would have been in 1722, with the stock bailout. Additionally, as evidenced in Part Two, the naval stores operation would probably have been abandoned once it had exhausted the critical mass of raw materials at hand. It would appear, judging by the apparently incomplete kiln installation evidenced by the stone circle, that the project was abandoned, rather than merely exhausted and relocated. Ironically, the *Bubble Act*, born at the company's instigation, became one of the instruments of their own destruction. South Sea Company did carry on for more than 100 more years, until, in 1854, William E. Gladstone, Chancellor of the Exchequer, finally closed the books forever.

Part Four – Finally! The Truth Unveiled

Knowing the "where," and a little about the what, of the mystery, it is time to reveal the amazing story of Oak Island in light of its history. The surprising truth is that something of great value was once *manufactured* on the tiny island, not buried beneath it. Oak Island was not a repository of treasure, nor of ancient holy relics. Oak Island was the location of a commodity so important, so vital, that when in short supply even the greatest super powers of the day cringed.

There is no doubt in my mind – and I believe that my research demonstrates – that the so-called Money Pit was not a great spectacular treasure trove. This will be a bitter pill for some to swallow, I know. That so many people invested their lives and fortunes over these old factory ruins, strikes both a sad and ironic chord. Though the truth about Oak Island is perhaps less romantic, it is no less interesting. The pursuit of the little-known aspect of Nova Scotia's past and the *story* of the Oak Island mystery are equally interesting and both are to be treasured.

∞

We know about the resounding cries from the British government urging naval stores production. We have learned the critical need of a scarce and expensive product during the age of the wooden boat. My contention is that the Money Pit was none other than a ground kiln constructed to produce naval stores for use of either the British Admiralty and/or use by the South Sea Company in its triangular slave trade (naval stores was a commodity known to be to be manufactured by slaves and traded for slaves). We can see the similarities drawn between the Money Pit and kiln construction.

Let's review the "elements" of the mystery outlined in Part One not already dealt with.

First impressions

Immediately below the layer of flagstones was said by the lads to be an obvious shaft that had been backfilled. As R. V. Harris puts it, "on removing the stones, they saw they were entering the mouth of an old pit, or shaft, that had been filled up. The mouth was more than seven feet in diameter and the sides of the pit were of tough hard clay, but the earth with which it had been filled was loose and easily removed."[1] This pretty much describes the top of a tar kiln to a tee.

It simply defies geology that such an erratic and abrupt pre-arranged layer of material, consisting of a non-indigenous stone formation, would occur naturally within the overburden and that an obvious filled pit existed below. It also tells us that the Money Pit is NOT a natural sinkhole as sometimes presumed, but rather that it was determined by the hands of man.

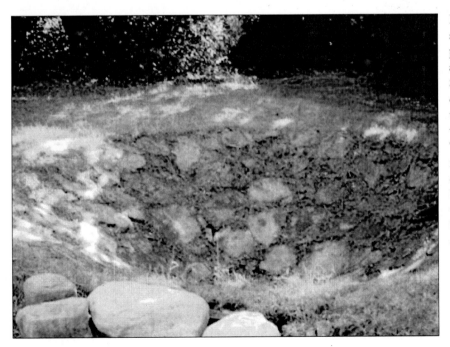

Fig. 4.1 – This picture shows flagstones atop a primitive Swedish Kiln at Trollskogen in Öland, Sweden. A typical circular depression due to subsidence is clearly visible atop the kiln. The photo compares favourably with the description furnished by the trio of lads upon discovery. Photo by Svenboatbuilder, Creative Commons.[2]

Figure 4.1, found on the Internet, clearly shows flagstones positioned atop a typical Scandinavian-style tar kiln. Telltale subsidence has developed as evidenced by the characteristic circular depression which forms atop a fired kiln over time.

Money Pit

An unmistakable set of similarities becomes immediately apparent when comparison is drawn between the Money Pit and the colonial tar-making process. As will be proven below, past evidence and depictions of the Money Pit works will mirror a classic tar-producing ground kiln.

Recall the instructions that these kilns be built on gently sloping land. It can be said with certainty that the Money Pit site had been originally constructed on the south side of a gently sloping knoll. The tar had to ooze its way down and out the outlet pipe by gravity, thus the importance of this type of landscape. For the same reason, most kilns of this era were made in the shape of a funnel. In a letter penned by S. C. Fraser dated June 19, 1895, to Mr. A. S. Lowden, the following is stated: "When the Money Pit fell in, it assumed the shape of a funnel nearly thirty feet [10 m] across at the top and to a point 113 feet below [34 m]."[3]

Fig. 4.2 (also Fig. 2.8 in Part Two) - "Tar Making in Bothnia," note the primitive winch device used to lower log billets into the pit. "Tar Making in Bothnia," *Penny Press* magazine, op. cit.

A block and tackle were said to be found dangling from a tree overhanging the Money Pit and imagined to be a remnant of either a treasure-hunting effort or even of a treasure burial. The purpose of the apparatus was most likely to act as a winch to lower a charge of pine billets into the Pit (see figure 4.2).

Inscribed Stone

To ensure that the inscribed stone is authentic, that it is of the period in question and not something planted closer to the time of its excavation (ca. 1805), I point to two clues of interest. Note the first two ciphers: inverted triangles, the second of which bears two strokes. Some examiners of the depictions of the ciphers have posited that the latter was struck in error and corrected with the first. This was no mistake. The first two characters taken together correspond to the old English "F." According to *Notes and Queries* dated September, 1855, "the double letter is only, in reality, a single capital F, formed of two strokes," customary in Old

English.[4] This was the way to pen a capital F, certainly ca. 1720, as innumerable documents exist to correlate the writing style of that time (figure 4.5).

The term "pounds" apparently inscribed on the stone certainly denotes the currency of the time (not, as some predictably hope, the weight of treasure), ca. 1720. The pound, shilling and pence would have been the currency expressed in accounts with the British Government in the early days of Nova Scotia. Given that the architects of Oak Island enterprise appear to have been English, it makes perfect sense that money would have been expressed in terms of pounds.

Apparently some paper money did circulate in the form of bills of credit or "Boston bills" in the first half of the 18th-century in Nova Scotia. This was largely owing to trade carried on between the British garrison at Annapolis Royal and Boston. For most of the early Nova Scotia settlers, however, the principal means of buying and selling was through simple barter, as in swapping one commodity with another.

There is yet another detail to be revealed in our little mystery of the stone, for never has the true meaning been revealed. Most equate the message with the notion that a couple of million pounds of loot lies in the ground below, but what if the whole thing might have meant something else entirely? When bathed in the new light that this was once a short-

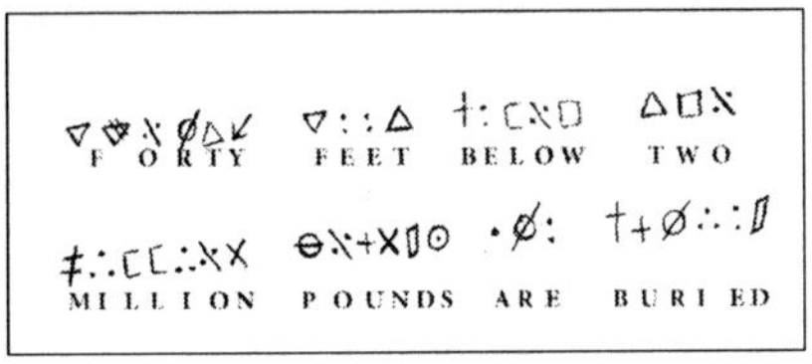

Fig. 4.3 (also Fig. 1.3) – Replica of the "inscribed stone" commissioned by author Darcy O'Connor in the mid 1980s for a television documentary drama for the ABC network. Photo courtesy Darcy O'Connor. Shared with the author and published with permission.

Fig. 4.4 (also Fig. 1.4) – The glyphs as rendered by A. T. Kempton in an unpublished manuscript, recorded by Richard Joltes, and overlaid with the widely accepted decoded message. NSARM. Kempton, A. T., story about Oak Island (typescript) Apr 28 1949. R. V. Harris Papers MG 1 vol 384, item 2364f-h.

Fig. 4.5 – Example of the old English style capital F as demonstrated by the signature of Sir Francis Nicholson.[5]

lived South Sea Company enterprise, one might now discern the real message this object was meant to convey.

Refer again to the clipping with the list of ventures categorized as "Companies Trading to America" eradicated as a result of the South Sea Bubble catastrophe in 1720. Among these was one proposal to import naval stores and, more importantly, the fact that these naval stores were to come from Virginia and Nova Scotia. Take notice once again the vast capitals of these projects and businesses demonstrated in figure 4.6.

The stone's riddle may be answered by thinking about the sixth entry which reads, "Ditto for importing naval stores from Nova Scotia and Virginia." The ditto of course refers to the whopping two-million-pounds capital allotted to the naval stores operation in Nova Scotia. Such huge amounts were typical in the "bubble" era of 1720; even the most promising of projects were outlandishly overcapitalized. In fact, there are only two known cases "where companies formed with a capital base of less than a million."[7] Further, refer to the two million pounds extended to South Sea Company following the stock calamity, as noted in Part Three.

My contention, therefore, is that the stone was likely engraved as a satirical pun of folly directed toward the ill-fated enterprise. Surely a mood of shock and forlornness prevailed when news of the shutdown arrived. The irony is almost palpable if the inscription laments the death of a once golden opportunity. It's not hard to imagine the stone's creator carving out a little English humor to make light of a bad turn of events – two million pounds of capital squandered and sunk into the ground just like the tar pit that lay below – a cynical tombstone bearing an epitaph immortalizing the fatality of the Oak Island naval stores business.

A. D. 1720.

America.
1, For settling the island of Santa Cruz in America.
2, — Ditto, for the islands of Blanco and Sal-Tortuga in Ditto.
3, Trade to the river Oronoko.
4, Ditto to Nova-Scotia, two millions.
5, Ditto to the Golden islands, Sir Robert Montgomery's.
6, Ditto for importing naval stores from Nova-Scotia and Virginia.

Fig. 4.6 (also Fig. 2.10) – Partial list of the overseas companies trading to America and ruined in the Bubble debacle.[6]

Flooding

The Money Pit was not, as supposed, linked to the shore works of Smith's Cove and as part of some elaborate flooding booby-trap. If the original builders had wanted to purposely rig the Money Pit, they could have more easily relied on a tunnel to the south beach rather than having dug 500 arduous feet (150 m) over to Smith's Cove.

The geology of the island's east drumlin (where the Money Pit is situated) consists of an underlying layer of gypsum/anhydrite. Overlaying this unstable mineral is a layer of glacial tumulus consisting of a mish-mash of sandy loam and boulder erratics. Subterranean groundwaters could easily pass through such materials and, in like manner seawater, could pervade these fractured channels.

Further evidence substantiating the possibility of natural groundwater/seawater infiltration of the subsoil strata came in the way of side-scan sonar studies, which had been run simultaneously with the dye tests mentioned in Part One. The results showed no indication whatsoever "of any sort of channel or 'drain' between the Pit area and the shoreline." Scientists summarized this finding by stating that "no direct connection to the surrounding ocean was found during the study."[8]

Box Drains

At the edge of the shore at Smith's Cove were discovered five covered channels which came to be known as "box drains." The drains were found to have fanned out much like the fingers of a hand and appeared to converge at one central point. Each box drain consisted of a pair of parallel lines made of rock slabs which measured about 8 inches apart (20 cm), topped with a layer of flat stones. Just beyond the "finger," or box, drains as they are also known, was found a section of an earth mound, thought to be a dam.

J. B. McCully, a member of both the Oak Island Association and the Truro syndicate of 1849-50, lets us know that "at the beach ... we found flag stones made in the form of drains and covered with a kind of grass, not the growth of this country, and the outer rind of the cocoa nut [sic]." He goes on to add, "by the way, the remains of an old dam was seen outside of the place where we found the drain and tunnel at the shore."[9]

Many have speculated that the box drains were actually part of a flooding mechanism deliberately hooked up to a main tunnel designed to sabotage any breach of the Money Pit. The more probable answer lies wrapped up in the conclusions of Mike Harmon and Rodney Snedeker entitled: "Seven Elements to the Production of Tar" listed in Appendix B. According to the archaeologists, not all tar kilns were single drain structures, simply stating that, "occasionally multiple trench drains were dug."[10] The box drains weren't there to let sea water in but to let something drain out. That something was pine tar which exuded from kiln #2, otherwise known as the Cave-in Pit site.

The earth mound found outside the box drains was explained away as a cofferdam built to restrain the sea during construction. This may have been the case in part, but not in entirety. The "old dam" which Mc-

Fig, 4.7 – Map of Oak Island's east end showing the box drain structure at Smith's Cove, etc. However, we must note that object no. 9 is refuted. Image from *Buried Treasure*, prospectus of the Oak Island Treasure Company, 1893. MG 12, 75 D4A. Beaton Institute, Cape Breton University.

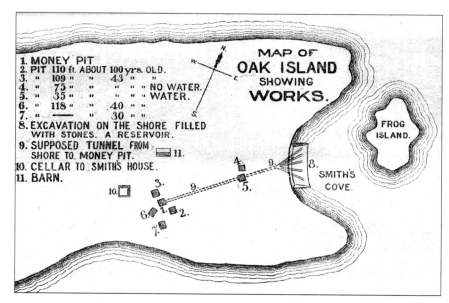

1. MONEY PIT
2. PIT 110 ft. ABOUT 100 yrs. OLD.
3. " 109 " " 43 " "
4. " 75 " " " " " NO WATER.
5. " 35 " " " " " WATER.
6. " 118 " " 40 " "
7. " ——— " 30 " "
8. EXCAVATION ON THE SHORE FILLED WITH STONES. A RESERVOIR.
9. SUPPOSED TUNNEL FROM SHORE TO MONEY PIT.
10. CELLAR TO SMITHS HOUSE.
11. BARN.

MAP OF OAK ISLAND SHOWING WORKS.

FROG ISLAND.

SMITH'S COVE.

Cully described was not solely a dam or cofferdam but an outer mound typical of many excavated kiln sites.

The sketch in figure 4.8 depicts a single-drain style tar kiln complete with the typically associated ditch and mound encircling the main kiln. The ditch and mound found their use as a conduit that served to channel escaping tar into the tar hold, or collection pit. Harmon and Snedeker explain:

> On the outer perimeter a ditch or hole was dug and the trench [or trenches] drained into this location. This ditch was usually around six feet in depth. Barrels or troughs would be placed in the ditch to allow for the collection of the tar. An outer ditch may have been dug to encircle the kiln and collect tar running off of the kiln's outer surface.[11]

But as the reason for differing drains constructions is presently uncertain, one can only speculate why these two styles may be found. Mike Harmon did offer two suggestions as to why multiple drains may have been used at some sites, and I would offer a third:

1) If one drain got clogged (due to the viscous nature of pine tar) there would be other outlets or drains to facilitate the outflow.

2) Multiple drains could also allow one to get the tar out of the kiln faster.

3) My personal belief is that within the Smith's Cove area of Oak Island, a cluster of kilns may have been concentrated (or planned) in a relatively small area. Thus, excessive tar runoff could be directed via the fan-like box drains to a common collection ditch.

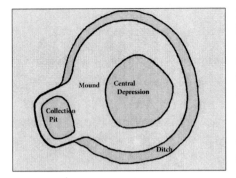

Fig. 4.8 – Kiln planning view showing elements as described by archaeologists Harmon and Snedeker. Note the typical mound and ditch around the kiln's outer perimeter. At times an additional ditch (and thus mound) could have been built as well. This correlates with to McCully's report of a dam, just beyond the box drain structure. Illustration by the author.

Harmon is a professional archaeologist who has excavated many tar kilns in North Carolina in the course of his career. If anybody knew about old tar kilns, Mike was definitely the one to ask. When we talked about naval stores production in relation to the Oak Island works, I asked if he would mind perusing my manuscript, perhaps with a follow up email with his comments. This he did, and the words that came back were sweet to behold.

Mike's letter stated:

Joy,

I enjoyed talking with you this morning. I can now see that you have indeed raised some interesting ideas that nobody else has yet ventured, and have certainly done your "homework." I would like to read the rest of your draft as time permits.

I have skimmed what I think are the relevant sections and I follow what you are saying....

I agree with your interpretation of multiple drains from what we discussed this morning.

Mike Harmon

∞

If what J. B. McCully saw was really once was an outer kiln mound (as opposed to being a dam to hold back seawater), that would imply that the inner box drain structure would have been originally built on dry ground (considering that tar was collected there as well). But that would translate to a hike in sea level of a couple of feet, or more, within a time span of almost 300 years. Is that possible? It is indeed, according to Natural Resources Canada, citing several scientists who support this claim. The department states that "evidence of transgression is indicated by enhanced erosion along many Atlantic Canadian beaches, and inun-

1998 high-tide level

1743 high-tide level

Fig. 4.9 – The photo at left, taken at Fortress Louisbourg, Nova Scotia, clearly demonstrates sea level rise since the 18th century. Photo by Ambrose MacNeil, courtesy Natural Resources Canada, 2006.

dation of terrestrial peat deposits and trees."[12] Sea level in the Atlantic region has risen approximately 30 cm. or better over the past century alone.

Coconut Fibre

It is true that coconut husk may have made for good dunnage back then; however, this was not the intended purpose within the Oak Island setting. As alluded to in Part Two, the coir was more likely a form of packing turf, to ensure the kiln stayed air-tight to prevent as well as stifle fire flare-ups.

Referring back to our description of kiln construction in Part Two, we are reminded that turf, mud and clay were needed as packing all around the kiln because it was absolutely essential that it be airtight (with the exception of the drainage spout affixed to the kiln's bottom from which oozed the pine tar). If air were allowed to enter the kiln un-controlled, the kiln would erupt in flames, spoiling the batch. Therefore, in all likelihood, the coconut husks functioned as the "turf," or packing, so crucially required for sealing in a smoldering tar kiln.

Coconut husk, or fibre retrieved from the Money Pit was said to be the same material found in great abundance at Smith's Cove, where the Cave-in Pit is located. Note, further, that Smith's Cove and the Money Pit were the only two locations on Oak Island at which coconut fibre has ever been found (with the exception of a small amount reported by Fred Nolan on his property). The implication is, therefore, that both areas could well have been former ground kiln sites.

This makes sense. There were, in all probability, two or more kilns; of course a quantity of this coconut material would have been found at each site, in this case, the Money Pit and Cave-in Pit. Records show that bushels of the coconut fibre were removed and piled in stacks like haycocks along shore at Smith's Cove (where the Cave-in Pit is closely situated).

And given that other ground kiln related evidence is shared by both sites (i.e., evidence of combustion, commonality of sloping landform, etc.), it is fair to say that two kilns are more likely to have been fired with a third being laid out – but not activated – on the island's opposite end. The South Sea Company's triangular trade routes (i.e., England, Caribbean, Nova Scotia) certainly gave them access to plenty of coconut husk.

The Cave-in Pit

"Hello Paul, I believe similar instructions used to create the Money Pit may have just been located!" I barked out excitedly over the telephone to fellow researcher Paul Wroclawski.

"Both the written directions and a sketch of the same is housed in the Canadian Archives in Ottawa. While I was able to obtain the written portion from another source, the sketch is still forthcoming. At any rate, I'll run this by you, and let's see if you can see any similarities.

I proceeded to read off the instructions used by Jonathon Bridger, Surveyor General of His Majesty's Woods in America, dated 1706:

> In May, June, July, & August, the tar tree may be prepared.... Cut
> it down in the middle – and split it into pieces 4 inches square, in
> proper lengths for the Pit.... The Pit – eight foot deep twenty foot wide
> at top, sloping towards the bottom. There the spout must be fixed for
> carrying the tar to the barrel-bung and sleepers must be laid across
> the bottom to lay the wood on and raise the wood as soon as possible
> end-ways, that being the natural way of the pores the turpentine [tar]
> will the sooner be forced out to the tar Wood with less heat ... etc.[13]

"So what do you think Paul, does this sound familiar to you at all?" hoping at best that he might ascertain some connection as I did. But I ended up getting more than I bargained for, as the unexpected but pleasant answer came back rather struck me like a slap in the face.

"Joy, do you realize what you just described to me?" he said as if he had come to some other resolution of the facts.

"The design of the Money Pit...?" I reiterated somewhat quizzically.

"You just described the Cave-in Pit exactly!!" he shot back.

It took a couple of seconds for the words to sink in, at which time I blurted out, "Oh My God, there could be another kiln on that island!"

"There may even be more," he joked, leaving me with one last mystery to grapple with before our conversation ended. That something else appears to have been tar kiln number 2, and the facts seem consistent with this premise.

Harmon and Snedeker identify several elements of kiln location in the Coastal Plain (U.S.), stating that kilns were most often constructed on low-lying ridges and knolls whose changes in topography are so subtle that they often don't appear on the USGS maps. Kilns are often found near seasonal drainages, and older kilns are often found near permanent drainages. While current vegetation is not an accurate reflection of historic vegetation, Harmon and Snedeker note that areas which are presently planted in longleaf pine are likely to have been pine forests in the past as well. Finally, based on their research in the Coastal Plain of North Carolina, Harmon and Snedeker note that tar kilns are likely to cluster. This suggests that one section of forest was harvested and worked at a time, resulting in several kilns in the same general area. Where one kiln is found, additional kilns are likely.[14] Multiple kilns may have once dotted Oak Island's landscape.

∞

The Cave-in Pit was built on a gentle sloping hill just like the Money Pit, but along the opposite north portion of the eastern drumlin. You may recall that hilly landform was important to facilitate the outflow of the viscous pine tar exuding from the kiln.

Chappell's Vault

The *Farmer's Library and Monthly Journal of Agriculture* (1847) contained an essay detailing the tar-making process and mentions why cement can sometimes be found within these kilns:

> In the course of one or two days it [tar] will begin to "run" from the trough (when the plug must be removed), into the tar-hole [cement vault], which is usually spacious enough to contain ten or fifteen barrels, and from which it is bailed out into prepared barrels made pretty much after the fashion of turpentine barrels, but with large bung-holes, into which a bucket funnel is placed to fill the barrel. Then it is ready for market."[15]

Parchment

The parchment debate rages on between those who think the parchment was a legitimate find and a clue, and those who favour a conspiracy to plant the scrap of a document. But how and why would any documents find their way to the subterranean depths of Oak Island, and what in-

Fig. 4.10 (also figure 2.9) – Nineteenth-century photo of tar-making. Note the worker in the foreground is ladling tar from a cistern (tar hold), at his feet to a barrel, which in turn vents tar into a crude box funnel on its way to a waiting barrel. In the background is another worker tending the turf capping the kiln.

Note that immediately behind the upright barrel is a cribbing that restrains the ground kiln. "Sweating out tar from Pine Wood in the turf covered Tar Kiln, North Carolina." Underwood and Underwood, New York. Courtesy of the author.

formation might they have contained? One explanation was offered by a Lunenburg area gentleman by the name of Earl N. Pentz. Appearing in the *Bridgewater Bulletin* August 12, 1981, Mr. Pentz wrote an article saying that not only could he explain the parchment but also claimed that a distant kin cached away a total of three chests on Oak Island.

He made further allegations of South Sea Company involvement and also that slavery was a central component to the story, as I have suggested previously. He has also fixed the date close to my offering, that being 1720. Although Mr. Pentz did not connect the naval stores evidence and, therefore, has differing thoughts about the Money Pit than I, he nevertheless did offer striking claims that deserved another look.

Pentz remembered the stories about Oak Island his aunt used to tell him growing up, but as a youngster he didn't take much notice. When he started digging into his family background, however, Pentz says he accidentally stumbled upon a remarkable family connection to Oak Island. His research led him to believe that a great-great uncle was directly involved there.[16]

"Much of what you read about Oak Island does not go back far enough," Earl commented, noting that, "actually from 1716 to 1719, Oak Island was taking shape as a well-planned community."[17]

Mr. Pentz claimed that a mysterious great-great uncle, was not only working for the South Sea Company, but was also actively involved in the Oak Island settlement. According to Mr. Pentz (in the *Bridgewater Bulletin*), the South Sea Company "floundered because of an imposed tax on importing slaves and a restriction on the number of shiploads of slaves that could be transported to the Americas." He also believed that Oak Island was being developed between 1716 and 1720 as a supply center and holding depot (underground) to pen slaves bound for the Americas.

"It makes sense," Earl said, "with a great number of slaves all that you would have to guard would be a small opening."[18] Although he makes no claim to knowing whether or not caves were used for holding slaves before the bubble burst on the South Sea Company, he is sure that his great-great uncle was involved in the slave trade and at some point placed three trunks (chests) at some location on the island.[19] Believed only to be family papers, the contents, he claims, would be of little value as a treasure find. Mr. Pentz has borne some criticism for lack of documentation.

The newspaper account piqued my interest, and I made the effort to find Earl Pentz, but the search led me to the sad news that I was too late. Mr. Pentz, 75 of Lunenburg, had already died (2009). After a marathon of phone calling, and pretty much ready to give up, Earl's closest family relatives were found in a town bearing their surname, that being Pentz,

Nova Scotia. My enquiries were greeted with the warning to "keep a close eye on your records girl, mind they don't turn up missing." Evidently, just as Earl was coming forth with the proof found at the Nova Scotia Archives, the records vanished. The implication, of course, is that they had been stolen. One family member in particular was very bitter and sad, as she recalled the ridicule and anguish poor Earl suffered.

∞

Perhaps this tiny treasure (the piece of parchment) is a last surviving bit of documentation that leads to a shadowy family history, perhaps not. What the parchment had once been attached to is really anyone's guess – we are simply left in the dark to wonder – but an enterprise, the size of that which I am revealing, was bound to have a great deal of formal correspondence coming and going over a number of years. It is reasonable that remnants of correspondence, on vellum, be strewn about the site – perhaps disposed of in the fires of the kilns.

Stone Triangle

Because the triangle pointed directly to the Money Pit and precisely to true north (the North Star), many feel it was showing the way to the treasure. A more plausible explanation might be had if one were to view the triangle as something else; not as just a triangle but as a particular marker known as a benchmark. A benchmark is a surveyor's mark or symbol used as a point of reference for surveying (usually marking the starting or closing point). Given that benchmarks are set or affixed to a predetermined elevation and position, it cannot be a coincidence that the Oak Island triangle was found to bear in the direction of True North.

The notion that the stone triangle might have once been a surveyor's benchmark was brought up to surveyor Fred Nolan, in our phone conversation of May 2012. What better person to quiz on this subject than a man who has surveyed professionally for years and knows Oak Island like the back of his hand? As we chatted, my impression was that he was genuinely interested in the benchmark suggestion and at no time did he offer to disprove it. Fred knew that an 18th-century surveyor could, by following from his benchmark, establish a baseline and run off a survey. This would also imply then that it was not that the stone triangle was meant to point at the Money Pit, but rather the Money Pit was, by design, intentionally built on this survey line – all neat and according to a plan.

As briefly touched upon in both Part One and Part Three, a survey may have been conducted on Oak Island in those early times. British au-

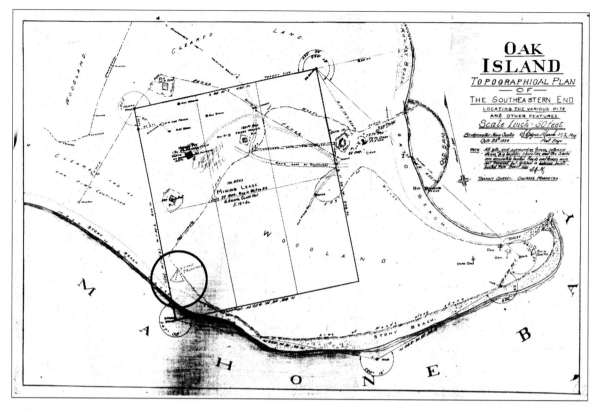

Fig. 4.11 (also Fig. 1.2) – The location of the benchmark (stone triangle) has been boldly circled, lower left. Oak Island-Topographical Map, 1934. S. Edgar March. MG 12.175 D.2A. Beaton Institute, Cape Breton University.

thorities realized that this virgin land had to be properly carved up and populated if they wished to maintain and strengthen their foothold in the western world. The following excerpt underscores the government's interest to initiate surveys and relates to us what was being decided in 1719:

> At Admiralty behest, not only was it then decided that the tightest restrictive regulations about tree-cutting should be extended to Nova Scotia, but in addition that no lands should be granted there for settlement until a total of 200,000 acres of woodland [had been] marked out by His Majesty's Surveyor General of the Woods in America in one or more parcels.[20]

In the case of Oak Island, surely the South Sea Company which operated there around 1720 would have been subject to a land survey prior to start-up. That stone triangle could well have marked the very starting point and, therefore, benchmark of the Oak Island works – had it survived.

Sadly, after having endured for centuries, the stone triangle has been obliterated, victim to the ravages of time and human interference. The last word on this mysterious icon of Oak Island history is summed up in a letter found among the M. R. Chappell files (likely from R. V. Harris), dated August 1, 1966, which bewails:

> Had a call from W. L. Johnson of Vancouver, "visited Oak Island the previous day, found it devastated." [...] The triangle on the south shore has entirely disappeared. I called C. P. Roper and Johnson spoke to him. He said the triangle undoubtedly was very old. Both agreed it was the work of an old sailor and the key to the mystery, not an accident.[21]

The Heart-shaped Stone

A call to David Blankenship (resident and son of treasure hunter, Dan Blankenship) quickly cleared up some misconceptions about the stone. "The stone only weighs about fifteen pounds and is about the size of a dinner plate," he informed me. (The stone was later weighed with an accurate scale and found to be exactly 9 pounds (4 kg)). The thought of the stone being an anchor went out the window, and the Knights Templar squirrelling away church icons seemed just a little far-fetched. Perhaps there is a better way to explain how the heart-shaped stone fits into the scheme of things.

An interesting theory, coined by Sidney Martin II, in a letter sent to M. R. Chappell (dated September 4, 1971) stated that "the heart stone may have served a very practical purpose as a plumb-bob to establish the vertical during construction of the shaft...." The heart shape is perfectly suited to this purpose as a line around each lobe would not slip, due to the expanding diameter and knotted at the cleft, which would prove a perfectly centered suspension point. This is true of no other shape which, without grooves or holes, would allow a line to slip. The point of the heart, of course, would indicate the descending vertical.

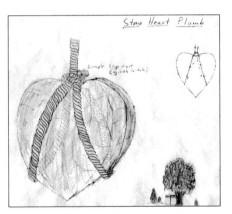

Fig. 4.12 – A sketch prepared by Sidney Martin II to demonstrate his point. The diagram gives a good depiction of how, by virtue of the stone's shape, cordage could be easily affixed. Perhaps this may explain why the stone was rendered in the shape of a heart. Stone Heart Plumb Sketch, n.d. MG 12, 75 D2A Folio 6. Beaton Institute, Cape Breton University.

The U-shaped Structure and the Wooden Sled

Another argument made for the presence of multiple kilns is the curious U-shaped structure found on the island's northeast side at Smith's Cove. As previously mentioned, it was unearthed by Dan Blankenship and Triton Alliance Ltd. during their excavations of 1970. The structure measured in excess of 45 feet (13 m) on its northern side, the front about 65 feet (20 m), and the southern side was found to be over 30 feet (10 m) in length.

If we glance at the wooden timbers just over the gentleman's shoulder to the left in figure 4.13, the answer finally comes into view. It turns out that most tar kilns needed to be shorn up given that they were usually built on a sloping embankment. Improper, or lack of, reinforcement around the kiln's base could lead to serious landslips, which threatened not only the workers, but could damage the tar output area. Hence, it was important that an adequate structural support and bracing system be implemented. This compares favourably with the u-shaped structure on Oak Island.

And then there was that odd little wooden box mentioned earlier as the box-sled, discovered only three feet below the u-shaped structure. The wooden box is identical to an apparatus used in tar-making called a bucket funnel which conveyed the tar into barrels or sometimes directly into a catch basin (tar hold). Referring to figure 4.13, we can see the process in action, whereby the gentleman first dips the raw tar from a cement tar hold and puts it in the barrel. Next, the tar is left to course out into the bucket funnel allowing a controlled flow to run down and fill up the second barrel via a bung hole.

The bevelled section of the box can now be easily explained as well. It was slanted at only one end because it had to slip under the hole where the tar was let out, thus reducing tar spills from escaping and being slopped onto the ground.

From the photos we may also glean the probable usage of the dowel-like piece found plugging one side of the wooden box. Figure 4.18 is a close-up of the bucket funnel and reveals that the bored-out holes flanking either side of the wooden box were in all probability sockets whereby a spindle could be inserted on each side. This would in turn function as a support mechanism to prop up the bucket funnel and secure it in place as the tar flowed over its interior.

The usage for the bucket funnel is explicitly mentioned and described as it pertained to pine tar manufacture in the 1847 *Journal of Agriculture*: "[tar] is bailed out into prepared barrels made pretty much after the

Fig. 4.13 (also 2.9) top left – Underwood and Underwood, New York. Courtesy of the author.

Fig. 4.14 top right – Dan Blankenship and an unidentified man atop the u-shaped structure. Photo by JimPickerell, Trition photo courtesy of Les MacPhie.

Fig. 4.15 bottom left – Aerial view of the excavation site exposing what is presumed to be an old slipway. Oak Island, 1969-1971. Photographer unknown. 81-566-5646. Beaton Institute, Cape Breton University.

Fig. 4.16 (also 1.12) bottom right – Oak Island, 1969-1971. Photographer unknown. 81-563-5643. Beaton Institute, Cape Breton University.

Fig. 4.17 (also 1.13) top – Box "sled" uncovered from below the u-shaped structure by Dan Blankenship in 1970. Triton photo courtesy of Les Mac-Phie.

Figure 4.18 lower left – A closer look at the 19th-century bucket funnel (detail from Fig. 4.15) reveals the likely purpose of the partially bored-out holes found on either side of the Smith's Cove wooden box artifact (4.19). Notice the use of the spindles and how they could be inserted into either side, then anchored into the earth so as to prop up and secure the object in place.

Fig. 4.19 lower right (detail) – Note the notch in the rear of the Oak Island box funnel.

fashion of turpentine barrels, but with large bung-holes, into which a bucket funnel is placed to fill the barrel. Then it is ready for market."[22]

An important, but apparently overlooked, clue hidden in plain sight was that little notch carved into the back end of the Smith's Cove wooden box. Sometimes what may be perceived of least significance may turn out to be the greatest lead. If this wooden box was indeed a bucket funnel, then one would expect to find a small exit point allowing the issuing tar to be let out. The whole purpose of using a bucket funnel was of course to direct a steady but controlled flow of the tar into a barrel. Clearly and without doubt such an orifice was found on the end of the wooden box (figure 4.19). An object whose purpose was previously obscured is now explained. No doubt can now exist that our little wooden box artifact served its days as a bucket funnel for use in Smith's Cove.

To verify this postulation that the wooden box found at Smith's Cove may have been a bucket funnel, I again consulted archaeologist Mike Harmon in South Carolina. Eventually, the following favourable report came back to me: (Note: The image he refers to is the old tar kiln photo pictured in figure 4.13 above).

Joy,

You are not bothering me. I almost responded yesterday, but...

I've never actually seen a bucket funnel because this is the sort of thing that is rarely preserved. I've seen the 19th century image before and see some physical similarities between the 2 examples

JOY A. STEELE

esp. considering there is at least a century time difference between them, and the Oak Island operation seems to have been more massive than most I have seen. I would expect the trough to be a little longer though.

I think your interpretation is very reasonable esp. considering the earlier evidence you have put forth.

Good luck with the book and keep me posted. Thanks, Mike

It was only when this reply came that I fully realized what a rare and precious artifact Dan Blankenship had stumbled onto back in 1970. The remarkable state of preservation in which the object was found was no doubt owing to its having been saturated in pine tar and then subsequent burial under several feet of earth. This simple little contraption once used in tar-making yielded up a big piece of the puzzle. Its secrets lent great weight to the fact that naval stores were probably not just produced at the Money Pit site, but that Smith's Cove too may have been a second area of production, where the object was found in situ.

The Megalithic Cross and the Headstone

I can't help but speculate a little more about the cross and confess to being more than a little fascinated by its orientation at about 55° north. Recall the CME medal (shown again below). Long a powerful symbol of Christian faiths, the cross is normally depicted in the vertical position. There are, however a number of uses of what is known as a *portate* cross, a diagonal cross, from the Latin *portare* "to carry." This would be the angle if the cross was borne diagonally over the shoulder, as so often depicted in illustrations of the Crucifixion story.

While I have not been able to acsertain if SPG used this symbolism in its 18th-century incarnation, I find the connection between the megalithic cross on Oak Island and the use of the portate cross by SPG's modern incarnation – the Christian Methodist Episcopal Church – to be compelling. Here are the ingredients of the mystery: a proselytizing organization with access to an abundance of slave labour and under the influence of a global enterprise on a tiny island.

The construction of a monolith this size must have been extremely labour-intensive, built by a large and coordinated workforce or team of individuals. Under the naval stores theory, and armed with the knowledge that it was the South Sea Company who set up shop here by 1720, I suggest the SPG was responsible. Acting in concert with the South Sea Company, such an operation might be undertaken even in such a desolate setting – both parties had the motive and means (including a royal charter). It would not be a stretch to suppose that the company took advantage of their human cargo, forcing them to toil on the workings on Oak Island and possibly the construction of the cross.

I leave it to readers to draw their own conclusions.

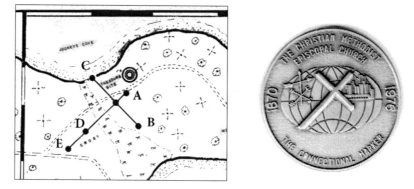

Fig. 4.20 – Detail from figure 1.14, showing the location and position of the megalithic cross on Oak Island. Plot plan by Fred Nolan, courtesy of the author. Note again the compass delineation of approximately 55° north and its similarity with the position of the *portate* cross on the CME (of which SPG was the predecessor) medallion in Fig. 4.21 (also Fig. 3.1).

Mark of the Arrow

The answer as to what the strange tree markings represented is already clear. We know that application of the broad arrow upon any object, whether it be a tiny nail or a tree, meant government ownership. We also know about the Crown's emphasis and insistence on surveys to hurry along settlement in Nova Scotia. One survey method used in the 18th century was triangulation. As implied by its name, triangulation makes use of three points of reference to determine survey data. Therefore, if the values of certain elements of a triangle are known, then the remaining unknown values of the triangle can be computed trigonometrically. Positions of survey stations (vertices) may then be calculated. Nowadays, we use electronic distance measuring equipment for such horizontal control surveys, but before such technologies, triangulation was the principal method, especially for hilly terrain like that on the island's east drumlin.

According to the Licensed Surveyors Regulations, "...a conspicuous tree shall be selected for reference, connected with the traverse, and marked with a broad arrow and a distinguishing letter and number."

JOY A. STEELE

Thus in the figure above, the "6" identifies the tree's location/position and also that it was claimed as Crown property by virtue of the mark of the broad arrow. The surveyor's initials are also sometimes carved into the mix for further identification purposes, so anyone seeing this strange muddle of carving for the first time would certainly find this to be puzzling.

The use of this particular survey technique may also explain why several stone piles were found on the island. The regulations go on to state that

> In localities where stone is available for cairns, posts shall be substituted for marked trees; such posts to be not less than six inches square, pointed at the top, placed firmly in the ground and protected by a cairn of stones three feet in diameter and three feet high.

Fig. 4.22 (also 1.18) – "Letters and figures" carved into a broad arrow tree.[23]

It can be no mere coincidence then, that Fred Nolan reported finding just such posts, or stakes, in an upright position (pointed end up and made of sandstone), in and around these stone piles. One stake was reportedly found by accident as Fred was tracing along the medial line of "the arrow-shaped triangle formed by the stone mounds."

What's more is that the Surveyor's Regulations go on to state that, "Each post shall have a broad arrow and distinguishing letter and number deeply cut in it." Mr. Nolan had revealed to author William Crooker that "some of the sandstone objects had marks and figures on them."

Stone Circle

Now that we have probed the possibility that both the Money Pit and the Cave-in Pit were tar kilns, it may be fairly suggested that there could have been others.

Readers will recall that research has informed me that there was a stone ring formation, about 40 feet in diameter (12 m), on Lot 5, (the northwest side of the island). This riddle threw me for a loop temporarily, but I knew that the circular structure had a familiar ring, pardon the pun. Eventually, it came to me that I had read that this was the very first thing the tar workers did to start construction of their ground kiln (but at that point, I did not known why). It all began with a framework of stones ringing the intended kiln area, laid not only as a digging guideline but, as was later discovered, to be an ingenious calculator of final tar output. Quite cleverly, the old-timers were able to measure roughly how much tar would be produced based on the kiln's diameter and depth. As one North Carolina producer described in 1847:

a circle being marked on the adjacent ground of from ten to thirty feet in diameter (3-10 m); the size depending entirely upon the number of barrels you design making from it: a diameter of thirty feet, and ten feet in height being the measure of a kiln of three hundred barrels.[24]

Mr. Nolan, in my last telephone interview with him, was asked point blank if there was a circle of stones found on Lot. 5. After a short pause he responded guardedly, saying, "there was something like that," but he did not commit himself to giving out more information. No one could blame him; after all this was someone else's lot now, and it was gathered from our conversation that he and that owner, Robert Young, were still in some sort of partner relationship with regard to the search for treasure.

That multiple kilns may have once dotted the Oak Island landscape is further strongly supported by archaeological study. Archaeologists Mike Harmon and Rodney Snedeker, who carried out extensive research on tar kilns in the coastal plains of North Carolina, were able to identify several common elements (see Appendix B). Among their conclusions, they found that tar kilns are likely to be found in clusters. This suggests that "a section of forest was harvested and worked at a time, resulting in several kilns in the same general area. Where one kiln is found they note that additional kilns are likely."[25]

Charred Wood

Combustion in some form had to have taken place to create the artifact. This supports evidence of possible kiln activity. Charcoal is the residue or by-product left after a kiln is fired. And in fact abundant charcoal residue was noted especially near the top layers of the Money Pit. Accounts varied from between 10 and 50 feet (3 and 15 m) as to the depth that the charcoal was encountered.

Even nowadays, outdoor enthusiasts still happen upon the remains of these ground kilns, mimicking the account given by the trio of lads in our story: "Hikers in some of North Carolina's coastal forests often run across the remains of tar kilns. The most visible clue is an unexplained depression in the soil, with perhaps some signs of charcoal just below the surface."[26]

Pine Billet

The wood sample seen at the Nova Scotia Museum most definitely had been hewn and split into a small billet-like piece measuring 43 x 23 x 10.8 cm thickness, or just under a foot-and-a-half in length and 9 inches wide by 4 inches thick. The pine log sample has a solid provenance, having been extracted from the Money Pit by treasure hunter Robert Dunfield. Pine was the preferred type of wood used in tar kilns.

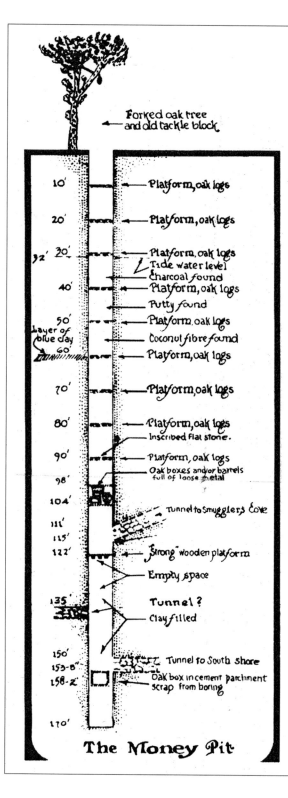

Forked oak tree
and old tackle block

10' — Platform, oak logs

20' — Platform, oak logs

32' 20' — Platform, oak logs
Tide water level
Charcoal found
40' — Platform, oak logs
Putty found
50' — Platform, oak logs
Layer of
blue clay Coconut fibre found
60' — Platform, oak logs

70' — Platform, oak logs

80' — Platform, oak logs
Inscribed flat stone.
90' — Platform, oak logs
Oak boxes and/or barrels
98' full of loose metal
104'
Tunnel to Smugglers Cove
111'
115'
122' — Strong wooden platform
— Empty space
135' Tunnel?
— Clay filled

150' Tunnel to South shore
153'-8"
158'-2" Oak box in cement parchment
scrap from boring

170'

The Money Pit

Part Five – The Final Pieces

Big Questions, Nagging Doubts – Also Solved

Now, some time must be spent to offer a reasonable explanation to account for the depths at which the Money Pit kiln and its associated sections have settled. While further proving that this was not the site of a treasure deposit, it will be shown that a complex series of events – seismic activity, geologic forces and human intervention – led to intense subsidence on the island's southeast side (that being the location of the Money Pit).

Figure 5.1 - This illustration, a clipping from an unidentified newspaper, illustrates the excavations of the Money Pit to that time. This account of the explorations has become the basis of contemporary expeditions. "Canada's Treasure Island," Newspaper, February 21, 1971. MG 12, 75 D2A Folio 7 (detail). Beaton Institute, Cape Breton University.

The main constituents found in or near the Money Pit and their respective depths may be summarized from figure 5.1:

– Two feet (60 cm) of overburden[1] underlain by a layer of flagstones.

– From 10 to 30 feet (3-10 m), layers of logs at 10-foot (3 m) intervals.

– A mark every 10 feet (3 m), (i.e., at 40 feet a layer of charcoal, at 50 a layer of putty [clay] and at 60 feet a layer of coconut fiber [12, 15 and 18 m]).

– Between 80-90 feet (24-27 m) was found an inscribed stone.

– From 98 to 104 feet (30 to 32 m), oak casks thought to be filled with loose metal.

– At 126 feet (38 m), an iron obstruction was encountered.

– From 153-160 feet (46-49 m) was found crude lime mortar encasing a wooden box. A scrap of parchment was extracted from within this area as well. The structure became known as "Chappell's vault," called after its discoverer, William Chappell, in 1897.

– At 171 feet (52) was another section containing iron.

It can be no coincidence that the artifacts found in the Money Pit, listed above match exactly with the components of a classic Baltic style tar kiln after firing – the flat tamping stones, residual charcoal, clay, turfing material (coconut), a cask, a cement-encrusted vault (tar hold) and sections of iron. But if this was once a tar kiln, usually about 8-10 feet (2-3 m) deep, how do we explain such (apparently) deep and layered features within the Money Pit. It appears almost as if the Money Pit and contents were pulled apart.

What forces played a role to cause such a contortion of the kiln? It is certainly possible, through human intervention, unique geologic conditions and seismic activity in the vicinity contributed tens of metres to the structure's collapse.

Upon examination of the seismic history of Atlantic Canada, it is recorded that a number of earthquakes shook the shores of Oak Island in the past. According to a study by Professor J. H. L. Johnstone, records indicate that no less than 325 earthquakes occurred in the Northeastern United States and Eastern Canada during the period 1638-1929.

Professor Johnstone reports that:

[O]f those quakes, 104 were of intensity 5 or greater (Rossi-Forrel scale). The epicentres occur in the region N. Lat. 40.6° to 47.6° and W. Long. 64.8° to 79.6°. Seven of the earthquakes, viz. those of 1663,

1732, 1755, 1791, 1860, 1870, and 1925, had intensities from 8 to 10. It is probable that eighteen of these tremors were felt in Nova Scotia and New Brunswick.[2]

The geographical coordinates of Oak Island are Latitude 44.51 and Longitude 64.30, placing it within approximately 25 miles (40 km) of the epicenters.

From the information above, we learn that three very powerful earthquakes affected the island between our proposed date of original construction up to the point of discovery by the three lads (1720 and 1795, respectively). Moreover, this powerful set of quakes had their epicenters within relatively close proximity to Oak Island at magnitudes sufficient to shake buildings and crack foundations. But even such powerful seismic activity may not account for the intense subsidence.

A combination of strong earthquakes occurring in unison with unique soil conditions can exhibit a natural phenomenon known as "soil liquefaction." Earthquake-induced liquefaction occurs when vibrations or water pressure within a mass of soil cause the soil particles to lose contact with one another. As a result, the soil behaves like a liquid, has an inability to support weight and can flow down gentle slopes. This condition is usually temporary and is most often caused by an earthquake vibrating water-saturated fill or unconsolidated soil.[3]

Liquefaction potential depends on a number of conditions which include the nature of the soil, availability of groundwater and severity and duration of seismic activity. Oak Island, upon close examination, appears to meet most of (if not all) the criteria conducive to a liquefaction event.

Breaking it down

1. Loose sandy sediments or fill are generally regarded as the most sensitive to liquefaction.

M. R. Chappell describes the soil encountered while excavating the Money Pit as "a clay, bluish in colour, with gravel mixed to a depth of about ninety feet [27 m] or so; then a layer of soft sandstone, six or eight feet thick, and below this, a brown marl formation, and drilling shows solid rock at about two hundred feet."[4]

Traditionally, clayey soils were thought not to be susceptible to liquefaction. However, research which followed the 1999 earthquakes at Kocaeli (Turkey) and Chi-Chi (Taiwan), during the same year, has "identified a large number of cases where ground failure in silty and clayey soils containing more than 15% clay-size particles caused considerable damage to buildings."[5]

2. The presence of groundwater or moisture within the subsoil.

Moisture content analysis data pertaining to the Money Pit area appears to be scarce. Fortunately however, one report labelled "Hole 43" located 180' [55 m] northeast of the Money Pit bearing same or similar soil characteristics was recorded by Dan Blankenship in 1967, giving some indication of the moisture content. Dan states that, "50' – 101' – [15-31 m] Softer layer of blue clay without too many stones. Clay could be worked by hand. Quite moist but not wet."[6]

3. An earthquake of Richter magnitude 5 or greater is necessary to induce liquefaction.

It has already been shown that several earthquakes beyond that level have affected Oak Island with three of those being of high magnitude. The greater the earthquake, the more likely soil liquefaction is to occur. Based on research carried out by Youd and Perkins (1987):

> For larger earthquakes, liquefaction has a greater likelihood of occurrence and will be found at greater distances from the epicenter. Liquefaction has been documented up to 170 miles (274 km) from the epicenter of an earthquake (1977 Romanian earthquake, magnitude 7.2).[7]

There are four types of ground failure which commonly result from liquefaction, with the emphasis on the last: loss of bearing strength, ground oscillation, lateral-spread landslides and flow landslides. Gentle slopes, such as where the Money Pit was originally built, may fail as the liquefied soils and overlying materials move down slope.

∞

Another consideration which may contribute in part to the Money Pit area disintegration lies in its natural geology. The underlying bedrock is composed of limestone and gypsum which are susceptible to dissolution in water and are associated with the formation of cavities.

Fig. 5.2 – Illustration of flow landslide phenomenon.

The following description of the island's geology was once mailed to me by the late Graham Harris, mining engineer and author of many books on Oak Island. In his writings, he brought to light very insightful information about the unique geology to be found on the southeastern end of the island and how solution

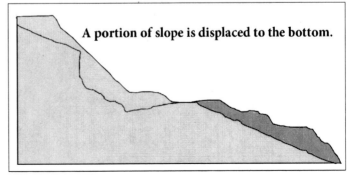

A portion of slope is displaced to the bottom.

caverns form. Mr. Harris wrote that:[8]

> Oak Island, Nova Scotia, is a product of the last Ice Age. Geologically the island is a drumlin, that is a mound of glacial moraine, composed of what is known as clay till, plastered upon the underlying surface over which the ice advanced and then subsequently retreated. Typically a drumlin possesses an oval shape, with its longer axis oriented in the prevailing direction of ice movement.

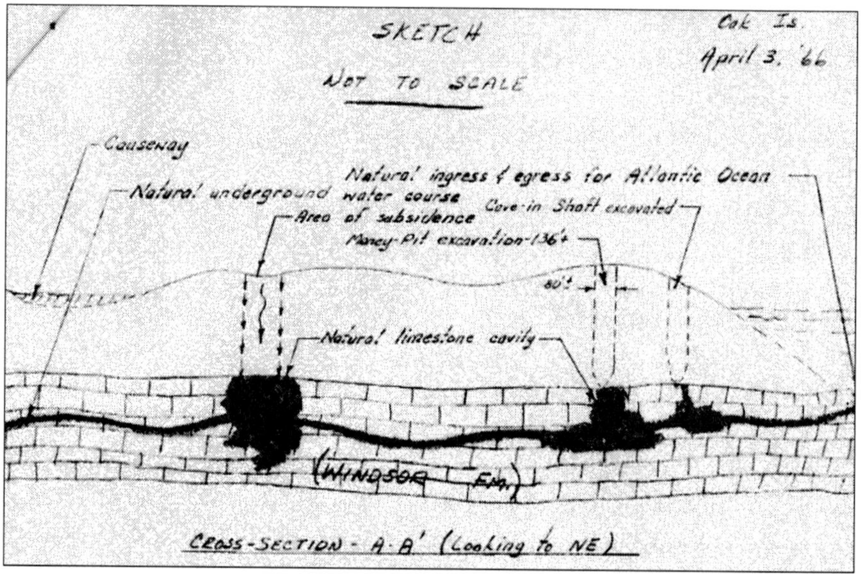

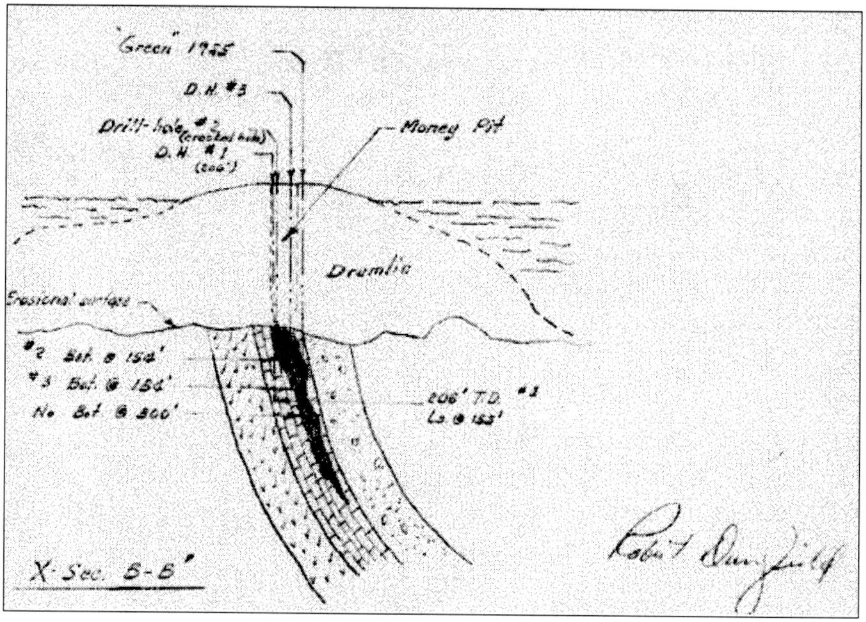

Fig. 5.3 and 5.4 – Sketches by Robert Dunfield (geologist and treasure hunter on Oak Island) showing the probable presence of natural cavities in the bedrock below the the island. Courtesy of Robert Dunfield Jr., with thanks to Jo Atherton, Oak Island Treasure Forum.

Slate bedrock is encountered at shallow depth at the western end of the island, and may be observed as outcrops on the adjacent mainland. Gypsum/anhydrite has been proved at a depth of about 200 feet [61 m] at the island's eastern end, in the vicinity of what is now known as the Money Pit.

The basal slate rock of the region originated during late Silurian or early Devonian periods approximately 400 million years ago. The overlying gypsum/anhydrite was deposited some 50 million years later during the ensuing Carboniferous, and generally mantles the slate where present at lower elevations, though some intervening limestone is occasionally encountered. Intense evaporation, associated with an increasingly torrid climate, concentrated the salts in the waters of the Carboniferous ocean, precipitating them within arms of the sea that had become isolated from the main body of water. Following deposition of the gypsum/anhydrite there is little in the geological record to suggest activity of any note to have occurred, until the onset of the Quaternary Ice Ages that terminated some 10,000 years ago. The geological evidence suggests the gypsum/anhydrite is confined to a localized depression, or pocket, within the slate bedrock surface.

With increasing evaporation, the first salt to be precipitated from sea water is calcium carbonate (or limestone—$CaCO_3$), the next is calcium sulphate (or anhydrite—$CaSO_4$) and, thirdly sodium chloride (or salt—$NaCl$). Anhydrite is the most interesting of these materials as it can hydrate to its allied form, gypsum ($CaSO_4.2H_2O$), by absorbing molecules of water in accordance with the following chemical equation which is fully reversible:

$$CaSO_4 + 2H_2O = CaSO_4.2H_2O$$
(Anhydrite) (Water) (Gypsum)

The degree of alteration of anhydrite into gypsum, and the reverse process whereby gypsum is transformed into anhydrite, depends on physical factors such as inter-particle pressure, temperature, and access to free water. Gypsum and anhydrite may be considered similar as they possess an identical chemistry. Any variation in their physical properties is dependent on the physics of their in-situ environment, which controls the equilibrium implied by the above equation.... Because of the chemistry of the solution mechanism, gypsum/anhydrite is far more soluble in salt water than in fresh.[8]

∞

It is not difficult to suppose that some slippage and subsidence may have occurred in the vicinity of the Money Pit kiln site. Ironically, many skeptics of the Oak Island story have theorized that the Money Pit was nothing more than a natural sinkhole. Ironic, because although the Money Pit didn't start its life as a sinkhole, but rather a tar pit, it WAS surely destined to become one at some point in its future.

Lastly, it can be said with certainty that the hand of man had intervened to contribute to considerable subsidence in the Money Pit area. In 1861, the Oak Island Association attempted to drive a lateral tunnel into the Money Pit which resulted in the collapse of the bottom of the shaft into what was likely a natural cavern underneath. Estimates ranging from a drop of 14 feet [4 m] to tens of feet have been suggested, with the latter being more realistic. The testimony of Samuel C. Fraser, a worker and witness to a great cave-in, wrote of a tremendous amount of lumber lost down the void, suggesting that the pit had crashed down to a considerable depth. In his 1895 letter to a Mr. A. S. Lowden, Fraser states that:

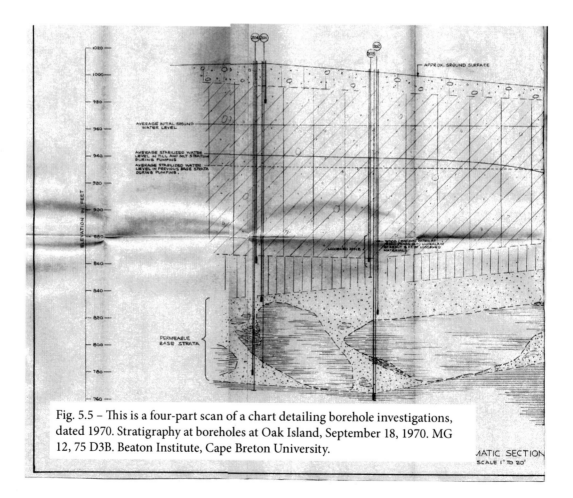

Fig. 5.5 – This is a four-part scan of a chart detailing borehole investigations, dated 1970. Stratigraphy at boreholes at Oak Island, September 18, 1970. MG 12, 75 D3B. Beaton Institute, Cape Breton University.

JOY A. STEELE

...I saw every sign of the cataclysm that was about to take place and refused to go into the money pit in time to save my own life and the men that would be with me. When the pit fell down I was there and I with George Mitchell, threw a line down as far as it was open from the top when the subsidence ended, – it was open 113 feet from the top. Now do read and mark this: As I told you before, there went down ten thousand feet of lumber – board measure – the cribbing of the old money pit.[9]

In summary, it is possible to ascertain how the Money Pit kiln became contorted and stretched to such depths. The conclusion is based both on events involving human intervention and natural phenomenon including repeated powerful earthquakes, possible soil liquefaction/landslides resulting from those quakes and unique geologic features on Oak Island's east end.

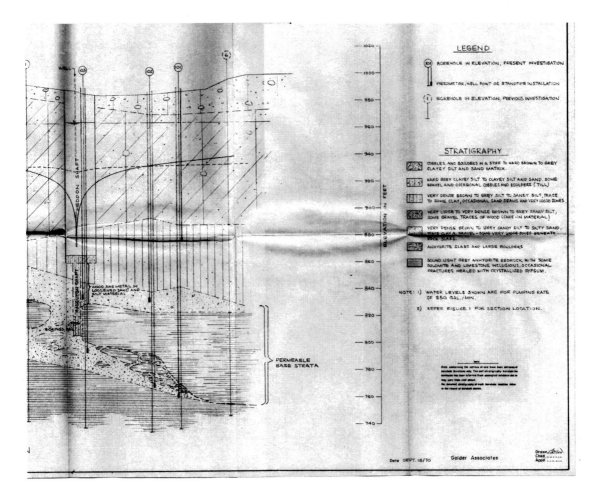

∞

Upon discovery in 1795, the three boys stumbled onto what they thought was the scene of a bygone treasure deposit. Understandably, they made an unfortunate misjudgement of the clues; in reality, they came upon the ruins of an old naval stores operation. What looked like the glory hole was merely a time-worn, weather-beaten tar kiln in the aftermath of somewhat intense seismic activity over the course of 75 years. By this time too, the subsidence associated with a ground kiln had contributed to the puzzling strata they encountered (depression at top, then flat stones followed by layers of wood down to about 30 feet (10 m)).

Subsequent treasure operations probed deeper into the pit, revealing the extent of the subterranean deformity which had occurred (e.g., scattered layers of charcoal, clay and coconut turfing. The bottom of the main part of the kiln was probably around the 100-foot (30 m) mark by 1850, judging by the position of what was believed to be a cask located there. The depth of the tar vault was not known at the time as it was not discovered until 1897. But, by 1861, it must have dropped some tens of feet in the occurrence of a great collapse; perhaps the effects of undermining by a tunnel driven from a nearby 118-foot shaft (36 m). Eventually, it would come to rest at depth between 153 and 160 feet (47-49 m).

Besides several seismic episodes and interference by man, soil and groundwater conditions on Oak Island bear characteristics that appear to be conducive to earthquake induced liquefaction. This in turn may have caused secondary effects such as flow failure landslides (figure 5.2). It is then possible that landslide debris could have tumbled downslope, burying part of the main kiln and tar hole. However, while the phenomenon of soil liquefaction occurrence around the Money Pit seems promising, it remains only a hypothesis based on mere remnants of rather scanty field data. It is, therefore, recommended that further testing be carried out such as basic particle size and shape analysis and an assessment as to the degree of ground saturation typical to the Money Pit site.

Parting Thoughts

If you go back to the very beginning of this book you may recall the legend stating that, in the year 1720, strange lights described as bonfires were burning on the island. Those fires we may now explain as being the kilns flaming up. Kilns were usually initially fired as evening came on (presumably because it is less windy), and were reported to be quite the creepy spectacle. As one account tells it, "you pass ... and which resemble burning volcanoes on a small scale ... surrounded by an unearthly set of black figures in human shape, thrusting long pikes into the agonizing structure."[10]

The legend also tells us that the mysterious fires and goings on stopped abruptly, as if whoever was there made a hasty departure. A newspaper was a rare thing in Nova Scotia prior to the founding of Halifax in 1749, but if they could read the headlines that were flying around Europe in 1720, Nova Scotians would be horrified to learn that the demise of the Oak Island enterprise was only the tip of the iceberg. The economic collapse had spurred on more than a few people to suicide and reduced good families to street beggars, had at the same time turned harlots to socialites; everything it seemed was topsy-turvy. Misery was rife and life was misery.

But the people of Western Shore, Nova Scotia, can take heart, because they can still look just beyond their doorsteps at one of the most beautiful seascapes on this continent. Instead of gazing at unsightly skyscrapers, which might have today littered these shores if a commercial metropolis had followed the investments poured into the area, we still enjoy the pristine beauty in small town Nova Scotia, oblivious to what nearly happened there. Just imagine, this place could have been the prosperous Halifax of its time; but nearly three decades earlier. Furthermore, Western Shore folks can now take great pride knowing that Oak Island really is a great historical and archaeological

Fig. 5.6 – Burning a tar kiln in North Carolina. From "Piny Woods of North Carolina." *Harper's New Monthly Magazine* vol. 14, no. 84 (May 1857): 744. Courtesy of Cornell University Library, Making of America Digital Collection.

feather in the Canadian cap. In my estimation, the fact that the South Sea Company operated on Nova Scotia shores, making a product our history says little about, accomplished with slave labour on the island as early as 1720, makes this a place to treasure.

New group to trumpet Oak Island

By BEVERLEY WARE
South Shore Bureau

BRIDGEWATER — Joy Steele couldn't believe her eyes when old silver coins spilled from her cousin's satchel onto the floor.

He was a diver and had taken the coins from a ship that sank off the coast of Cape Breton in 1725. That's the moment the 10-year-old's love for shipwrecks, treasure and intrigue were born.

Today, 37 years later, Ms. Steele is a founding member of a new group called the Friends of Oak Island Society, formed to promote the island following the dissolution last month of the Oak Island Tourism Society.

The new society is not yet registered, but founding members are in the process of organizing their first meeting.

"Entire fortunes amounting to the tune of millions of dollars have been squandered to crack this mystery, but she still stubbornly holds her secrets," Ms. Steele said of the curious island in Western Shore and why it intrigues her so.

She was the sole person to vote against dissolving the Oak Island Tourism Society during its final meeting in early December. She said she was concerned about the fallout for local businesses, how to keep the story alive for tourists and what would happen with recovered artifacts.

But those issues are now for the new society to worry about.

Its mandate is to promote Oak Island's history both locally and abroad by displaying research and artifacts recovered from the island in an interpretive centre. Those items are now in the hands of the Chester Municipal Heritage Society, but they will move back to the Gold River-Western Shore area once an interpretation centre has been built.

Ms. Steele is sure public interest in the mystery of Oak Island is still vibrant, as evidenced through Internet forums, new books that are still coming off the presses and two new documentaries.

"The real pot of gold at the end of the rainbow is the history and knowledge that can be gleaned from the island and then shared with the general public," she said.

Oak Island landowner and treasure hunter Dan Blankenship and the four Michigan men who have invested with him are still awaiting approval from the province for their treasure trove licence. They have said the search for treasure will resume as soon as they have that licence.

Ms. Steele predicts that the mo-

Digging to resume for long-rumoured treasure on Oak Island

HALIFAX (CP) — The hunt for buried treasure on Nova Scotia's Oak Island is about to resume for the first time in more than a decade.

Four Americans plan to spend at least $200,000 to drill next month at a spot they believe holds the key to unlocking a mystery that has foiled treasure hunters for more than 200 years.

Local partner Dan Blankenship says he and his four associates will focus their efforts on an underground shaft called Borehole 10X.

"I made some very, very important discoveries that were not followed diligently," Blankenship said of earlier exploration efforts.

For two centuries, treasure hunters have been drawn to the tiny windswept island by stories of pirate treasure buried in a booby-trapped shaft known as the Money Pit.

Theories suggest the pit is home to everything from Captain Kidd's pirate booty and the Holy Grail, to the lost jewels of Marie Antoinette and treasure plundered by Sir Francis Drake from French and Spanish ships.

At least six people have died trying to find treasure here since 1795, when three boys found a concealed shaft beneath a big oak tree.

Blankenship said he's found evidence of wire, chain and low-carbon steel in bedrock 60 metres below the surface.

He wouldn't say if he has a specific schedule work to be done.

2007

Members angered, saddened by society shutdown

By ADAM JACOBS
ajacobs@southshorenow.ca

WESTERN SHORE — Last week's news that the Oak Island Tourism Society is planning to cease its existence took many people by surprise.

The public response has been that of disbelief, anger and sadness.

The society has scheduled a meeting for 2 p.m., December 7 at the Oak Island Resort and Spa at which point the membership will be asked for its input and a decision will be made.

The news hasn't just had a local effect, however.

For more than 200 years the public has been following, arguably, the most intriguing treasure hunt the world over.

Since it formed in 2001, the society has helped provide the public with an inside look at the search, which is ongoing to this day.

John Henderson lives in New Hampshire.

A former member of the society, he has visited Oak Island every year since 2005.

"And I visited twice that year," he said. "I maintained about 12 memberships for family and friends (from 2004-2006) in those years as well as donated hundreds of dollars and many, many hours of my time helping the society."

He said he even paid for the cost of a portable bush hog to clear the island one year.

"At the time it was a privilege and an honour."

After some difficulty with the society, Mr. Henderson said he chose not to renew his membership, yet he still follows the island exploits closely.

In a letter to society members, communications director Danny Hennigar suggested two major reasons for the decision to dissolve the society.

The first reason is "lack of clear direction from majority landowners and treasure hunters of Oak Island Tours Inc. on whether or not we stand any reason chance at fulfilling our full ...

The second reason ... unable to ... Oak ...

... each year."

Mr. Henderson said those aren... sons enough.

"The society does not have to clo... doors given the minor issues of ... access or even getting a yearly venu... the event," he said. "Let us not forg... consultant's report which says a ... land interpretive centre would also ... with on island being only more idea...

"The two main reasons outline... your membership letter are not ... more than petty and shifting blam... you cannot get the vision realized, o... no longer interested in John Chataw... vision, then you should step aside and... others try. The Western Shore needs ... OITS, just as the OITS needs the Wes... Shore with both growing through ... tual co-operation."

For his part, Mr. Hennigar said ... an interview he would be happy to ... another group step forward should ... society fold.

Mr. Henderson is not alone in his ... taste for the society's decision.

Joy Steele, an avid researcher of Sou... Shore history and a member of the so... ety, said she is worried about what w... be lost should the society close.

The artifacts held by the society wou... be transferred to the Chester Munici... pal Heritage Society, and in all likel... hood would be on display in the Villag... of Chester "instead of keeping the... in Western Shore where they most cer... tainly belong," Ms Steele said. "Thi... means that the local community will suf... fer greatly, for one, by the loss and insul... of artifacts being removed out from their... very noses.

"Secondly, the economic impact on... the community will be very hard felt ... because the annual Explore Oak Island ... Days will cease to exist which o... bolstered economic spendin...

Ms Steele is also ... bylaw that d... by ...

Man-Hour Output

PRODUCTION per man-hour (nonfarm) in the second quart... 102.4% of the 1967 average (ro... 109.2% in the first quarter, th... partment reports.

Let the treasure hunt begin

[If there was ever a clos... hors...]

www.southshorenow.ca

weekly • 3,798 print readers weekly

$1.55 +HST

...TERPRISE

...SDAY, JULY 20, 2010 • 135th year, No. 29

TO THE EDITOR

In other words, common sense dictates that there is nothing to lose, but loads to gain for us all. With proceeds from the treasure itself coupled with museum revenues, the government coffers would overflow like a "cash cornucopia." Imagine if you can, the boost and spinoffs for the local economy learning and knowledge to be gleaned for posterity's sake and most importantly, the benefits all of us would reap — no child would ever go to bed hungry in this province again.

Therefore, the government needs to stop dragging its collective heels and get on with business. Together, we can prevent this golden opportunity from slipping away from us and I invite the public to join our efforts. I vote to let the treasure hunt begin and let us all be instrumental to write the final chapter to this incredible story.

JOY STEELE
Director, Friends of Oak Island Society
Sydney Forks, Cape Breton

Treasure trove licence for Oak Island
Government promises new act soon

By ADAM JACOBS

WESTERN SHORE — After two years of waiting, Dan Blankenship and his partnership group have finally received a treasure trove licence.

Not that it's going to do them much good,

the longtime treasure hunter said.

The licence was one of five granted by the province late last week. Each licence expires on December 31, 2010, about five months from now.

"They hold us up for two years and then they give us five months?" Mr. Blankenship said. "After that who knows what they are

meaning to do? I don't know if they know what it means."

Just days before the province granted the licences it announced it was repealing the Treasure Trove Act, meaning these five licences are the last to be granted by the province under that legislation.

See LICENCE, A3

Oak Island T...
Still Eludes Band
Of Dogged Sear...

Some 'Crazy' Little...
Prod Diggers C
Mull Taking H...

By D'ARCY O'C...
Staff Reporter of THE WALL...
OAK ISLAND, Nova...
small piece of rusty wire

Keep Oak Island mystery alive

Nova Scotia's most impor-
[...] cal assets and potentially
[...] argest tourist attractions
[...] essarily in a good way.
[...] nd, a small parcel of land
[...] vince's South Shore, is the
[...] of the world's biggest and
[...] ring archeological myster-
[...] as the world's longest-
[...] easure hunts. For more

thus far those efforts have met with
numerous blocks from government
red tape and private interests. M

MAIL STAR

The Chronicle Herald

Oak Islan[...]
Still Elu[...]
Of Dogg[...]

Some 'Craz[...]
Prod Di[...]
Mull Tak[...]

Americans set to drill at Oak Island

By D'A[...]
[...] Reporter of [...]
OAK ISLAND, [...]
small piece of rust[...]
Blankenship shakes [...]
the things like this [...]
keep me going."

For 10 years [...]
1969 assisted by fell[...]
dian-U.S. syndicate [...]
Ltd.—has been tryi[...]
world's intriguing [...]
300 or 400 years ago [...]
shaft into this island [...]
ward, probably left [...]
is the works and c[...]
flooding system to [...]
Triton partners h[...]
which nearly $100,0[...]
ship's own money, tr[...]

The best guesse[...]
treasures. And the b[...]
think, still may be th[...]
island 45 miles west [...]
tia's Mahone Bay.

This newspaper r[...]
land treasure hunt f[...]
time. Triton Allianc[...]
either to unravel the [...]
1970 or pack it in. To [...]
solved it nor given t[...]
triguing clues like b[...]
drawn, according to [...]
keep turning up [...]

Fiber, Gold and Iron

The original deep [...]
stumbled on by two s[...]
come to be known [...]
Since its discovery, [...]
been made to find wh[...]
workings. Franklin D. [...]
ner in one syndicate [...]
in 1909.

No treasure has b[...]
years, however, drill [...]
island have uncovere[...]
en quantities of coc[...]

Sha[...] [...]rgeted

By BEV[...]
South [...]

you don't have to go digging
on fabled Oak Island

land, there's a potential for 49 per
cent in taxes to be paid on it," he said.
[...] to pay a 49 per cent tax on
[...] [...]land.

Voluntary Planning, a citizens' policy forum, expressed concern that the
Treasure Trove Act does not ade-
quately protect underwater heritage.
[...]ain said in an interview

Local partner Dan Blankenship says he and his four American associates will focus their
Oak Island efforts on an underground shaft called Borehole 10X.   (TIM KROCHAK / Staff)

POST, FRIDAY, APRIL 25, 1975

ROUNDUP

[...]cial Land Survey
[...] Oak Island Find[...]

(CP) [...]
[...] a major
[...] to locate
[...]hone Bay [...]

High Honor

HALIFAX (CP) — Most Rev.
W. W. Davis, Metropolitan of
the Ecclesiastical Province of
Canada and Anglican Arch-
bishop of the Diocese of Nova
Scotia, will be made a Freeman
of the City, May 6, Mayor Ed-
mund Morris said today.

Archbishop Davis, who retires
this summer, will be one of six
persons given the honor, the
city's highest. The last was
former Lieutenant-Governor H.
P. MacKeen in 1968.

then, he has been [...]
vinced that the treasure, or a good por[...]
it, lies under his several hundred yards [...]
away from the Money Pit. He has done litt[...]
drilling and digging. Instead, he has spent [...]
the past few years surveying the island, [...]
starting from ancient stone markers he [...]
thinks were erected by whoever buried any [...]
treasure. He won't talk in any detail about [...]
what he thinks he has determined. But he [...]
says he has "almost reconstructed the origi[...]
nal treasure map" and soon will begin dig[...]
ging in "key locations."

"I'm close, really close," he says, adding
that he will "solve the Oak Island mystery
this summer."

Oak Island hasn't been altogether a los-
ing proposition. The Nova Scotia provincial
government began issuing guided tours of
the island in 1972. Last summer, 14,000 people from as far away as Australia and the
Soviet Union came to peer into the water-
filled craters that testify to all the years of
treasure digging. This year, 20,000 visitors,
at $1.50 a head, are expected to tour the is-

---

to discover one of the real
treasures of Nova Scotia

ACADIAN

7 SEAS
LIGHT RUM

7 SEAS RUM

WHITE, LIGHT OR DARK

...from the land
where Rum is known and appreciated
at its treasured best!

Four-decade treasure hunt
yields good yarns, but no gold

RICHARD FOOT
CanWest News Service
OAK ISLAND, N.S.

He is almost as much a
mystery as the con-
founding Island that
has been his obsession for
39 years.

Here at the site of the
world's longest treasure
hunt, where for two cen-
turies people have specu-
lated that Oak Island holds
some enchanting historical
prize, the big question now
revolves less around the
property itself than around
Dan Blankenship.

How could this sane and
perceptive man — a Second
World War veteran, an ac-
complished businessman, a
humane and charming per-
son — spend half of his life
and all of his money chasing
an enigma off the Nova Scotia coast, a fabled pot of treasure that may not even exist?

Since 1965, Blankenship
has poured his considerable
energy and his life savings
into an unsuccessful quest
for lost gold. He is 80 now,
still strong and confident,
but weathered with age.

He and his wife Jane live
in a simple bungalow at one
end of the island, where
Blankenship entertains visitors in a ramshackle base-
ment office overflowing
with filing cabinets, maps
and dusty documents.

Piles of paper, not gold,
are the main result of his
decades-long pursuit.

Blankenship knows his
life is winding down and his
search is nearing an end.

He says he never imag-
ined, when he first came to
this island, that he would
still be wrestling with its
riddles today.

"At the time, I figured I'd
find what I was looking for
in less than a year," he says.

Asked if he regrets devot-
ing his life to this unlikely,
single-minded mission, the
old treasure hunter turns

quiet for a moment.

"It's hard to say. It's hard
to say," he says softly. "I
don't know at times myself
what keeps me going."

Blankenship was working
as a contractor in Miami in
1965 when a Reader's
Digest article about an-
oovered pirate treasure
buried on Oak Island caught
his eye.

He became enthralled. A

man of ambition and
supreme self-confidence, he
declared to his wife: "Number one, there's treasure on
that island. Number two,
I'm going to be instrumental
in getting it off."

Blankenship bid farewell
to Florida, moved onto Oak
Island with his wife and
adult son, and dedicated
himself full-time to finding
the treasure.

For years he walked the island in search of under-
ground cavities with a
forked dowsing stick. He
sank dozens of shafts and
tunnels, some of them more
than 60 metres deep. He
waded through swamps, and
lived into underground caverns in scuba gear, nearly
killing himself when one of
the shafts collapsed on him.

Despite coming up empty
so far, Blankenship clings to
his belief that Oak Island is
the repository of shiploads
of lost Incan gold, brought
north by Spanish galleons
and hidden in a series of
complex tunnels and cav-
erns dug below the bedrock.

"I'm close, I'm very close,"
says Blankenship.

"You see, I just can't give
up on Oak Island. I'm way
past that point now."

For Dan Blankenship, X has never marked the spot.
Scott Dunlop/CanWest News Service

The instructions on how to make a tar kiln by John Bridger (1706) read off as follows:

Information & Directions for the Making of Tar & The choice of trees for the same as Finland.[1]

Trees – none with dead branches on top (a certain indication of decay of the tree) but flourishing full of limbs (tall trees seldom produce much tar). In May, June, July, August the tar tree may be prepared (or any month when sap is all up in the tree) depending on the Spring.

Two foot from the earth strip off the bark to eight foot up ---leave only a hand's breadth on the side with most limbs. Thus the tree must stand for two years. Cut it down & in the middle split it into pieces about four inches square, in proper lengths for the pit (no trees should be less than 12 inches in diameter).

The Pit – eight foot deep twenty foot wide at top, sloping towards the bottom. There the spout must be fix'd for carrying the tar to the barrel-bung and sleepers must be layed across the bottom to lay the wood on and raise the wood as soon as possible end-ways, that being the natural way of the pores the turpentine will the sooner be forced out to the Tar Wood with less heat. The Tar Wood may be raised seven foot above the earth. Great care must be taken in covering it, for if the air gets to the fire it will blow all up & burn the Tar. It must be cover'd with turf and sand very close and then with thin splinters of tar wood set on fire, put it into the pit which is generally three days in burning. If there are any knots, mix them with other wood, but not alone.

In Vasa in the same province they have another method where their Clay ground is, near the pitch pine tracts. In the spring they bark one part, the next another part &c until 4 years pass & the tree is cut down. The pit is made eight foot at the bottom 50 to 60 foot at the top. White pine bark is put on the inside to prevent Tar from running into the earth while burning. Tar wood is put end-ways in the Pit. Water is drained from tar in the barrel for it is always uppermost.

APPENDIX B

Seven Elements to the Production of Tar[2]

These are:

1) Proximity, Selection and Procurement of Fuel. Seasoned pine was the preferred fuel for tar kilns. In the South, longleaf pine was the main fuel source. Forest sections were normally cut or cleared in advance of tar kiln construction, allowing the wood to dry and season. Seasoned trees were then cut and split into pieces for easier stacking and waste materials, such as stumps and limbs, were stored separately for use as fuels.

2) Preparation of the Kiln Foundation. The ground surface was cleared in a circular area for the construction of the kiln. Soil was excavated to form a shallow circular depression, generally in between 15 and 25 feet in diameter. Clay was the preferred base for tar kilns, but kilns could also be built on sand. In sandy setting, the kiln floor was probably packed.

3) Trench Construction. A trench was dug from the center of the kiln through the outer perimeter. The function of this trench was to allow the tar to drain from the interior of the kiln to the outside where it could be collected and processed. The trench thus sloped downward from the interior to the exterior. A pipe was often placed in this trench and occasionally multiple trench drains were dug. On the outer perimeter a ditch or hole was dug and the trench drained into this location. This ditch was usually around six feet in depth. Barrels or troughs would be placed in the ditch to allow for the collection of the tar. An outer ditch may have been dug to encircle the kiln and collect tar running off of the kiln's outer surface.

4) Kiln Construction. The kiln was created by stacking the cut wood in a circular or octagonal fashion. Wood was stacked with the grain facing inward. The center of the kiln contained waste wood such as stumps and limbs and was used as a fuel source within the kiln. Twelve to 15 cords of wood were generally used in a kiln's construction. An opening was left at the top of the kiln. Kilns have been described as looking like "haystacks" and were generally between 10 and 15 feet in height.

5) Kiln Covering. The outer surface of the kiln was covered in earth, turf, and pine straw to dampen the fire once the kiln was ignited. Tar was created by allowing the dead wood in the kiln to burn at a low heat, hence a dampening cover which kept oxygen from the kiln fires was necessary.

6) Firing of the Kiln. Kilns were fired from the opening in their top. Once the fire had caught, this opening was covered with earth to prevent combustion. Long poles were used to poke holes through the sides of the kiln, beginning at the top and then moving toward the bottom as the kiln's firing proceeded. Referred to as "tempering the heat," the poles introduced oxygen to keep the fire from dying. Harmon and Snedeker note that tar making "was a smoky, dirty, and often hazardous occupation. If the burn proceeded too slowly, there was danger that the kiln could explode and hurt the operators. If the fire flared up, tar would be wasted." (Harmon and Snedeker 1997:148).

7) Collection of the Tar. By the second day of the firing the tar had begun to flow and would continue to flow for a period of four to five days. As the tar ran through the trench or pipe it exited the kiln into the ditch where it either drained into the barrel or a trough. In the latter instance, the tar would be collected from the trough and transferred to the barrel. Tar was collected day and night while the firing was on-going and a barrel of tar was normally collected per cord of wood in the kiln. As the tar flow slowed, on the sixth day after firing, additional dirt was thrown onto the kiln to smother the fire. Once the kiln had cooled, it was dismantled and charcoal was collected from its remnants.

Notes

Notes for Introduction

1. Drumlin is a geological formation – An elongated hill formed by glacial movement.

2. Darcy O'Connor cited Helen Creighton (1950) for this curse, in a post to Oak Island Treasure Forum.

3. Harris, R.V., *The Oak Island Mystery*, 4.

4. Malone, *Pine Trees and Politics*, x.

5. O'Brien, *Oak Island Unearthed*, 2014, 12-14.

6. A piezometer measures the pressure of a fluid or the compressibility of a substance. A tomograph makes an x-ray of a selected plane of a body. Bathymetry is the measurement of the depths of oceans, seas or other large bodies of water.

7. Three chapters in serial, January 2, 7 and 14, 1864, in *The British Colonist*.

8. Snow, *True Tales of Buried Treasure*. 1951, 23-24.

9. Longstreth, *To Nova Scotia*, 26.

10. Longstreth, 26-29.

11. Ibid.

12. Preston, "Death Trap Defies Treasure Seekers for Two Centuries," 1988.

13. (January 1965).

14. O'Connor, *The Secret Treasure of Oak Island*, 171-72.

15. O'Brien.

16. O'Connor interviewed Peggy Adams's mother in 1976.

17. O'Connor, 159.

Notes for Part One

1. O'Brien.

2. Sora, *The Lost Treasure of the Knights Templar*, 1999.

3. DesBrisay, *History of the County of Lunenburg*, 302.

4. Most accounts say 1803, but R. V. Harris says it was 1804. The group was active 1803-1805. It seems reasonable that a discovery at such a depth would have occurred late in their activity.

5. "Digging for Buried Treasure at Oak Island, Chester," the *Yarmouth Herald*, Thursday, July 10th, 1862, Vol. XII, No. 21. Differing accounts abound regarding when and where the stone was found; some say at 90 feet (27 m) while others say the stone was recovered at a depth of 80 feet (24 m). As the *Yarmouth Herald* article is based on the direct testimony of J. B. McCully, a depth of 80 feet (24 m), it is regarded by this author to be the most reliable.

6. *Halifax Sun and Advisor,* July 2, 1862.

7. O'Connor, personal communication.

8. "John Smith dies in Aug 1857." PANS MG 100 Volume 230 #32-33E microfiche 9809 – Descendants of the Smith and Floyd Families.

9. *British Colonist*, 2 January, 1864.

10. Harris, R. V., 19.

11. Many have presumed that the "Irish school master" mentioned by Reverend Kempton is one and the same with the Dalhousie professor, James Liechti. A recently discovered biography of James Liechti, written by historian and author P. B. Waite offers fresh details about this shadowy professor. For one thing, Waite states Liechti was Swiss, adding other interesting facts which cast serious doubt on his being the Irish school master. P. B. Waite recounts that: "At the same time as De Mille was appointed, James Liechti was hired as tutor in modern languages. Liechti was Swiss, a Lutheran, who taught French and German in the Halifax Grammar School for six years. He was liked by students, patient, kind, hardwork-ing. In 1883 he became McLeod professor of modern languages. He survived longer than any of the original old guard; he retired in 1906 to Lunenburg and lived until 1925." Waite, P. B., *The Lives of Dalhousie University*, 112.

12. Harris, R. V., 19.

13. Ibid., 19-20.

14. Ibid., 20.

15. Ibid.

16. Driscoll, *Doubloons*, 12.

17. Joltes, "History, Hoax, and Hype."

18. Due to the differences in the density of fresh water and seawater, fresh water floats in the upper part of the aquifer over seawater in the lower layer, often found beneath and sometimes the source of, potable water on small islands.

https://www.jircas.affric.go.jp/english/publication/highlights/2010/2010_32.html (accessed November 24, 2014).

19. Harris, R. V., 14.

20. Chappell, R. R., "Read, Think, and Reason," 6.

21. Ibid., 9.

22. Harris, R. V., 78.

23. Letter from M.R. Chappell to Dan Blankenship, January 3rd, 1975 (courtesy Beaton Institute). The test was done by A. Boake Roberts and Company Ltd., Analytical Chemists, London, England, who reported that they were "of the opinion that it is a cement which has been worked by man." Chappell, R. R., 13.

24. Harris, R. V., 114.

25. Chappell, R. R., 19.

26. Ibid.

27. Harris, R. V., 109.

28. Ibid.

29. Sora.

30. Harris and MacPhie, *Oak Island and Its Lost Treasure*, 114.

31. Crooker, *Oak Island Gold*, 173.

32. Ibid., 179.

33. "Sturt's Tree"-http://hay.nsw.gov.au/VisitHay/PlacestoVisit/SturtsMarkedTree/tabid/137/Default.aspx. Accessed 2014, (Australian gov. site).

34. Chappell, R. R., 5.

35. Ibid., 7.

36. Letter from R. V. Harris to W.L. Johnson, June 30, 1966. MG 12.75. Beaton Institute, Cape Breton University.

Notes for Part Two

1. "Britain's palladium" or My Lord Bolingbroke's "Welcome from France," by Joseph Brown.

2. *South Carolina Historical Magazine*, vol. 108, 181.

3. Oleoresin is a mixture of oils and resin (e.g., balsam).

4. Lightwood was so called because it was easy to light afire due to a high content of flammable resin in the wood. Earley, *Looking for Longleaf*, 86.

5. Ibid., 86.

6. Ward, "Naval Stores," 286-91.

7. Outland, *Tapping the Pines*, 9.

8. As a result of the monopoly, between the years 1689 and 1699 prices more than doubled from 5 pounds 15 shillings for twelve barrels, to 11 pounds. By 1703, the price doubled again to £22 for twelve barrels. Ibid., 9-10.

9. William Blathwayt, among the first appointees of Britain's Board of Trade, was reputed not only for his intelligence and shrewdness, but also for his wide knowledge in colonial matters. While he had scant personal knowledge of New England, his "eyes and ears" there had long been Edward Randolph.

10. "...it was generally recognized that the New England mast, of *pinus strobus,* resilient because of the extraordinary retention of 'the juices,' would remain serviceable for as long as twenty years more that the *pinus sylvestris,* the Scotch fir found in the forests of northern Europe." Malone, 6.

11. Malone, 6.

12. Outland, 12.

13. The Board of Trade at this time was called "The Council for Trade & Plantations," but later changed the name to "The Board of Trade." The Board of Trade had major responsibility for the colonial naval stores policy.

14. Outland, 12.

15. Factors were employed by most producers. The factor oversaw the unloading, inspecting and selling of naval stores once they arrived in port (Outland, 55).

16. England had imported 30,117 barrels of Swedish tar and pitch in 1701, but only 6,654 barrels arrived the following year. Ibid., 10.

17. Malone, 25.

18. By comparison, the wartime freight rate from New England was approximately £8 per ton. Exporters from the Baltic States paid only £2.

19. Malone, 25.

20. Malone, 27.

21. Malone, 33.

22. Dodson, *Alexander Spotswood.*

23. I cannot say with certainty what the "burning" effect was, nor why it was considered detrimental. Reference is also made to its adverse effects on elasticity.

24. C.O. 323, 7. No. 78, and 324, 10. pp. 100-106.

25. Cal. State Paps., America and West Indies – March 28th, 1717, v.29, 515i.

26. Ibid., 263-80.

27. Report on Canadian Archives. 1896. "Nova Scotia," 37. Ottawa: Queen's Printer.

28. Beamish. *A History of Nova Scotia or Acadia*, vol. 1, 393.

29. Ibid.

30. C.22, B.T.N.S. vol. 3.

31. Cal. State Paps., Col. (1717-1718), §543.

32. Aitken, and Easterbrook, *Canadian Economic History*, 190.

33. Bell, *The Foreign Protestants*, 44.

34. Barnard, and Guyot, *Johnson's Universal Cyclopaedia*, 599.

35. Ibid.

36. *The Broad Arrow Story*, 8.

37. Daniels and Kennedy, *Negotiated Empires*, 255.

38. Mayo, *John Wentworth*, 47.

39. Knittle, *Early Eighteenth Century Palatine Emigration*, 123.

40. Hammond, et al. *Transcripts from Ancient Documents*, 677.

41. Malone, 70.

42. Daniels and Kennedy, 255.

43. Malone, 95.

44. *Mark of Broad Arrow & Colonist's Hostility* - The Project Gutenberg eBook, American Merchant Ships and Sailors. Abbot, Willis J. (Illustrated by Ray Brown). http://www.gutenberg.org/files/15648/15648-h/15648-h.htm. April 18, 2005 [eBook #15648].

45 Manning, *New England Masts and the King's Broad Arrow*, ii.

46. Webster, *Acadia at the End of the Seventeenth Century*, 135.

47. Harris, R. V., 5.

48. Angus, *Big White: The Pine that Built a Nation*.

49. "In making pitch, round holes are dug in the earth near the tar kiln, five or six feet over, and about three feet deep; these holes are plastered with clay, which, when dry, are filled with tar, and set on fire. While it is burning it is kept continually stirring; when it is burnt enough (which they often try by dropping it into water) they then cover the hole, which extinguishes the fire, and before it cools it is put into barrels." Stephenson, *The Institute of Archaeology Notebook* – University of South Carolina, 8-9.

50. Lescarbot and Biggar, *Nova Francia*, 123.

51. Natural History of Shipworm, Teredo Navalis, *Biological Bulletin*, 260-82.

52. Earley, 88.

53. Malone, ix.

54. Bridger is referring to the Province of New York. Knittle, 123.

55. C.O. 324, 10. pp. 267-69.

56. These criteria are compiled from a number of sources, but chiefly paraphrased from: Skinner, "The Tar and Turpentine Business of North Carolina," 1847.

57. Stockholm tar was so-named originally because it was put aboard ships at Stockholm, Sweden. Eventually, the name stuck to all imported from that region and became synonymous with the best quality tar that could be bought in its day.

58. Manuscripts and Special Collections at The University of Nottingham holds a number of collections relating to the Portland family of Welbeck Abbey, the two most significant being the Portland (Welbeck) Collection and the Portland (London) Collection. The Welbeck collection consists of the personal and political papers of a number of members of the Portland family which had been part of the Library at Welbeck Abbey, Nottinghamshire.

William Arthur Henry Cavendish-Bentinck, 7th Duke of Portland (1893-1977) had control over a vast family archive. By his wish, it was divided between a number of repositories, chosen as appropriate to look after different elements within the archive. In 1986 the Portland papers from Welbeck Abbey were accepted by the nation in lieu of tax, and were allocated to the repositories where they had already been held for many years. The collection includes:

• Cavendish Family Papers (Dukes of Newcastle upon Tyne) which became part of the Portland family archive through the marriage of Lady Margaret Cavendish Harley to William Bentinck, 2nd Duke of Portland in 1734.

• 1st Earl of Portland (Pw A) Hans William Bentinck (1649-1709).

Of particular interest to this book:

• Harley Family Papers of a number of members of the Harley family including Sir Robert Harley (1579-1656), Sir Edward Harley (1624-1700), Robert Harley, 1st Earl of Oxford (1661-1724) and Thomas Wharton, 1st Marquess of Wharton (1648-1716) which came into the Portland family on the marriage of the 2nd Duke to Lady Margaret Cavendish Harley.

59. "Specie" is an 18th-century term for currency. "Paper" refers to stock issues.

60. "Arcadie" [sic] refers to Nova Scotia.

61. December 22, 1720; Portland MSS., V., 610.

62. MacNutt, *The Atlantic Provinces*, 16.

63. MacPherson, *Annals of Commerce*, 96.

64. Bell, 30, (with note): "On 17 April 1722 one finds the group begging for a hearing of their own case. On 20 Aug. 1723 some of the petitioners tried, apparently, to accelerate proceedings by affirming that one of their intentions was the production of hemp and other naval stores, and presenting certificates of their services at the conquest of 1710."

65. Waller, *Samuel Vetch, Colonial Enterpriser*, 281.

66. B.T.N.S. vol. 33, p. 35.

67. C.O. 152, 13 ff. 38, 39, 39v, 41v.

Notes for Part Three

1. "The Court of Madrid granted 'to her Britannic Majesty,' and to the Company of her subjects for that purpose; an *asiento* for supplying to the Spanish Colonies with 4,800 Africans yearly for 30 years." Mahon, *History of England*, 286.

2. Cwik, *The End of the British Slave Trade*.

3. Johnson and Smith, *Africans in America*, 68.

4. Ibid., 70.

5. West, *A Journal of a Mission to the Indians of the British Provinces*, 214.

6. Balen, *The Secret History of the South Sea Bubble*, 35.

7. Former Virginia Governor Alexander Spotswood (while standing before the Board of Trade in London) testified that he had made tar but had to give it up shortly after legislation in 1724 was changed in favour of the new style of concocting naval stores: "turpentining." Spotswood disliked this method, citing that too many trees were put to waste (as compared to the preferred ground kiln method he used in Virginia).

8. Detweiler et al., *Explorers to 1815*, 247.

9. *An Account of the Propagation of the Gospel in Foreign Parts*, 29.

10. Encyclopedia of African American History, 101.

11. Douglass, *A Summary ... of the First Planting*; Hochschild, *Bury the Chains*, 62-63.

12. Douglass. The South Sea Company contracted with the Royal African Company in 1721 for a supply of "3,600 negroes, two-thirds males, six-sevenths to be from 16 to 30 [years]. The other seventh to consist of equal numbers of boys and girls, none under 10 [years old]. The contracted price was £22. 10 s. Sterl. per piece for the Gold-Coast, Jackin, and Whidaw negroes; £18. 10 s. Sterl. for Angola slaves." Douglass states also that for some years the Company farmed out some of their *asiento* factories.

13. Collections of the Nova Scotia Historical Society – For the Years 1896-98, 6.

14. http://news.bbc.co.uk. "Church Appologises for Slave Trade." BBC News, February 8, 2006.

15. Porter, *Religion Versus Empire*, 21.

16. *Classified Digest of the Records of the Society for the Propagation of the Gospel.*

17. Konig, *Devising Liberty*, 282.

18. From O'Farrell.

19. Balen, 34.

20. Ibid., 70.

21 Carswell, *The South Sea Bubble*, 109-10.

22. Mahon, 267.

23. McCarthy, *A History of the Four Georges*, 217.

24. The only way to dissolve a company's charter was to bring a writ of Scire Facias against the said enterprise.

25. Capper, *The Port and Trade of London*, 113.

26. Realey, *The London Journal and its Authors*, 15.

27. MacKay, *Memoirs of Exrtraordinary Popular Delusions*, 114.

28. See the Portland Manuscripts.

29. Waller, 281.

30. Transcripts of Colonial Office Records, Nova Scotia, Gov. Phillips and Lt. Gov. Doucett, 1721. Nova Scotia "A" A13 (vol. 13), 1-4, microfilm reel C-9121.

31. December 22, 1720; Portland Mss., V. 610. *The South Sea Bubble, and the Numerous Fraudulent Projects to Which it Gave Rise in 1720*, 1825. 2nd ed. London: Thomas Boyd, 95-96.

32. Ibid.

Notes for Part Four

1. Harris, R. V., 8-9.

2. Photo by Svenboatbuilder. Creative Commons. http://en.wikipedia.org/wiki/Tar#/media/File:Tj%C3%A4rdal_092.jpg.

3. Letter of S. C. Fraser to A. S. Lowden, June 19, 1895. From the Chappell collection held at Beaton Institute, Nova Scotia. Mr. Fraser worked on the island for four years, including one year as foreman for the Halifax Company. Chappell, R. R., "Read, Think and Reason."

4. *Notes and Queries: A Medium of Inter-communication for Literary Men, Artists, Antiquaries, Genealogists, etc.*, vol. 12, London: George Bell, September, 1855, 170-71.

5. Windsor, *Narrative and Critical History of America*, 422.

6. MacPherson, 96.

7. Balen, 90.

8. Joltes.

9. *Yarmouth Herald*, July 10, 1862.

10. Joseph, Hamby and Long, *Historical Archaeology in Georgia*, 118.

11. Ibid.

12. Natural Resources Canada, "Climate and Climate-Related Trends and Projections," http://www.nrcan.gc.ca/environment/resources/publications/impacts-adaptation/reports/assessments/2008/10261 (Modified 2012-10-18).

13. Malone, 152.

14. Harmon and Snedeker, quoted in Joseph, Hamby and Long.

JOY A. STEELE

15. "As told by Mr. John MacLeod of Johnston, NC, himself a pine turpentine manufacturer for many years. MacLeod noted that the tar making method described is the same practiced as far back into antiquity as he has known." Skinner, 17.

16. The nameless man was the older brother of Pentz's great-great-grandfather Rudolf, "...a family legend about a great-great uncle [who] lost his life when he fell into a pit on Oak Island." He had "stored three chests containing the countess's manuscripts in the underground rooms but died trying to retrieve them." Morell. See note 4.19 below for more of Pentz's story.

17. Mossman, "No Treasure, just Family Papers," 1.

18. Ibid., 2.

19. Of the mysterious grandmother, Earl Pentz said she came from a line of blue-blooded royals and she had been locked in the so-called "Blue Tower of Copenhagen." Half expecting to see nothing of importance, I must say it was quite a surprise when a case was found concerning a lady of royal bloodline who had spent years imprisoned in the Blue Tower of Copenhagen. Her name was Leonora Christina (Countess Ulfeldt), one of the many children of King Christian IV of Denmark.

Leonora's troubles came in the wake of treasonous accusations hurled against her husband, Count Corfitz Ulfeldt. Her refusal to attest to Corfitz's alleged treachery saw poor Leonora locked away in the Blue Tower of Copenhagen where she languished for some 23 years before being released.

Being of strong mind and fierce resolve, Leonora was determined to carry on despite the gloomy and deplorable conditions she suffered throughout most of her confinement – sometimes she would be awakened by rats gnawing at her bedside candle – and she was denied even basic items such as writing materials. So great was her passion to put pen to paper, however, that on the sly she fashioned ink out of candle soot, her notepad from tatters of sugar bags, and her pen from a feather. Thusly she did write, but her autobiography and memoirs so painstakingly penned would only be published posthumously. Her efforts would not be in vain, however, because in years to follow she became somewhat of a Danish folk heroine, not to mention an icon to feminists. Her book many Scandinavian people might recognize by the name *Jammers Minde* literally, "a memory of lament."

That the mysterious granny may have been one-and-the-same as the indomitable daughter of a Danish King, Leonora Christina, is another story.

20. Bell, 44.

21. Letter from Chappell Files, August 1, 1966. It appears to be a memo from R. V. Harris. Courtesy Beaton Institute, Nova Scotia.

22. Skinner, 17.

23 "Sturt's Tree"-http://hay.nsw.gov.au/VisitHay/PlacestoVisit/SturtsMarkedTree/tabid/137/Default.aspx. Accessed 2014, (Australian gov. site).

24. Skinner, 17.

25. *Historical Archaeology in Georgia*, 119.

26. Earley, 91.

Notes for Part Five

1. Overburden is a mining term for the waste earth and rock covering a mineral deposit.

2. Johnstone, 227-37.

Regarding the Rossi-Forrel scale readings ranging from 8-10, the following is meant to give some inkling of those magnitudes. The effects may be described as follows:

> VIII. Very strong shock. Fall of chimneys. Cracks in the walls of buildings.
>
> IX. Extremely strong shock. Partial or total destruction of some buildings.
>
> X. Shock of extreme intensity. Great disaster, ruins, disturbance of the strata, fissures in the ground, rock falls from mountains.

3. Geology.com. "What is Liquefaction," http://geology.com/usgs/liquefaction/.

4. Letter from M. R. Chappell to John Quann, April 9, 1962, courtesy Beaton Institute.

5. Donahue, et al. *The Liquefaction Susceptibility, Resistance, and Response of Silty and Clayey Soils*, 2007.

6. Notes by Dan Blankenship on Becker Drilling Program, (Compiled by Les Mac Phie), pp. A1 – A4.

7. Black, et al. *Geology and Geologic Hazards*, 25.

8. Personal email from Graham Harris, quoting from his own book (Harris and McPhie), July 7, 2008.

"I'm including a copy of Appendix I "Why the Treasure was Lost" from *The Golden Reef of Sir William Phips*. This book covers Phips's exciting exploits of treasure-seeking, his involvement in conspiracy leading up to the revolution of 1688, and concludes with the loss of much of that treasure on Oak Island in April/May 1689. This summary may give you a better understanding of the geological backdrop regarding the loss of the treasure. If you feel inclined to read the book you might like to contact me again.

9. Letter Samuel C. Fraser to A. S. Lowden, June 15, 1895. (Courtesy Beaton Institute).

10. Earley, 94.

Notes for Appendix

1. Transcribed from Bridger, who printed these instructions in 1706. *Acts and Resolves, 1703-1707*, 646. In Finland, the practice was to dig the pit on a gentle slope, which Bridger did not mention. Where he wrote turpentine, he meant tar. Malone.

2. There are seven elements to the production of tar, as recorded by archaeologists Michael Harmon and Rodney Snedeker (1997: 147-48), as reprinted in Joseph, Hamby, & Long, 117-19.

References

Periodicals

Bridgewater Bulletin.

British Colonist.

The Colonist.

Halifax Sun and Advisor.

Harper's Weekly.

South Carolina Historical Magazine.

The Penny Magazine of the Society for the Diffusion of Useful Knowledge.

Reader's Digest.

The Yarmouth Herald.

Weekly Journal (London).

Primary and Unpublished Sources

B.T.N.S. vol. 33, p. 35.

Cal. State Paps., America and West Indies – March 28th, 1717, v.29, 515i.

Chappell, R. R. *Read, Think, and Reason* document, Beaton Institute.

C.22, B.T.N.S. vol.3.

C.O. 323, 7. Nos. 78, and 324, 10.

Collections of the Nova Scotia Historical Society.

"John Smith dies in Aug 1857." PANS MG 100 Volume 230 #32-33E microfiche 9809 – Descendants of the Smith and Floyd Families.

Kempton, A. T. (typescript) Apr 28 1949. PANS R. V. Harris Papers MG 1 vol 384, item 2364f-h.

The Portland Manuscripts.

Published Sources

Aitken, Hugh G. J. and W. T. Easterbrook. 1988. *Canadian Economic History*. Toronto: University of Toronto Press.

An Account of the Propagation of the Gospel in Foreign Parts. 1706. London: Joseph Downing.

Angus, Chris. 1992. *Big White: The Pine that Built a Nation*. American Forests, September-October.

Balen, Michael. 2003. *The Secret History of the South Sea Bubble*. New York: Fourth Estate and Harper Collins Publishers.

Barnard, Frederick A. P. and Arnold Guyot. 1890. *Johnson's Universal Cyclopaedia: A Scientific and Popular Treasury of Useful Knowledge*, vol. 1., pt. I. New York: A. J. Johnson & Co.

Beamish, Murdoch. 1865. *A History of Nova Scotia or Acadia*, vol. 1. Halifax: James Barnes.

Bell, Winthrop P. 1990. *The Foreign Protestants*, reprint ed., Mt. Allison University: Centre for Canadian Studies.

Black, Bill D., Barry J. Solomon and Kimm M. Harty. 1999. *Geology and Geologic Hazards*. Utah Special Study 96, Utah Geological.

The Broad Arrow Story. 1968. Nova Scotia Forest Products Association, Acadia University.

Capper, Charles. 1862. *The Port and Trade of London*. London: Smith, Elder and Company.

Carswell, John. 1993. *The South Sea Bubble*. Dover, NH: Alan Sutton Publishing.

"Church Apologises for Slave Trade." BBC News, February 8, 2006. http://news.bbc.co.uk.

Classified Digest of the Records of the Society for the Propagation of the Gospel in Foreign Parts 1701-1892, 5th ed. 1895. London: S.P.G.

Creighton, Helen. 1950. Folklore of Lunenburg County. National Museum of Canada. Bulletin no. 117, Anthropological Series no. 29.

Crooker, William S. 1993. *Oak Island Gold*. Halifax: Nimbus.

Cwik, Christian. N.d. *The End of the British Atlantic Slave Trade or the Beginning of the Big Slave Robbery, 1808-1850*. https://www.academia.edu/11903774/The_end_of_the_British_Atlantic_slave_trade_or_the_beginning_of_the_big_slave_robbery_1808-1850.

Daniels, Christine and Michael V. Kennedy. 2002. *Negotiated Empires: Centers and Peripheries in the Americas, 1500-1820*. New York: Routledge.

DesBrisay, Mather Byles. 1895. *History of the County of Lunenburg*, 2nd ed. Toronto: William Briggs.

Detweiler, Laurie and Ned Bustard, et. al. 2007. *Explorers to 1815 Teacher's Manual*, 2nd ed., USA: Veritas Press.

"Digging for Buried Treasure at Oak Island, Chester." 1862. *The Yarmouth Herald*, Thursday July 10th, Vol. XII, No. 21.

Dodson, Leonidas. 1932. *Alexander Spotwood*. Philadelphia: AMS Press.

Donahue, Jennifer L., Jonathan D. Bray and Michael F. Riemer. 2007. *The Liquefaction Susceptibility, Resistance, and Response of Silty and Clayey Soils*. Berkeley, CA: University of California Berkeley.

Douglass, William. 1755. *A Summary, Historical and Political, of the First Planting*. Boston, MA: R. Baldwin.

Driscoll, Charles B. 1930. *Doubloons*. New York: Farrar and Rinehart.

Earley, Lawrence S. 2004. *Looking for Longleaf: Fall and Rise of an American Forest*. Chapel Hill, NC: University of North Carolina Press.

Graves, Bill. 1928. Natural History of Shipworm, Teredo Navalis. *A Biological Bulletin*, vol. 55, no. 4, October. Woods Hole, MA: Marine Biological Library.

Hammond, Isaac W. and John S. Jenness, et al. 1885. *Transcripts from Ancient Documents in the English Archives in London – Part II*. New Hampshire: n.p.

Harris, Reginald V. 1967. *The Oak Island Mystery*, 2nd ed. Toronto: McGraw-Hill Ryerson.

Harris, Graham and Les MacPhie. 2005. *Oak Island And Its Lost Treasure*, 2nd ed. Halifax: Formac.

Hazlitt, William. 1825. Epistle to John Dryden, Esq. In *Select Poets of Great Britain*, 208-11. London: Tegg. http://books.google.ca/books?id=zCdDAQAAMAAJ&pg=PA210&lpg=PA210&dq=%22Safe+in+ourselves,+while+on+ourselves+we+stand%22&source=bl&ots=yaE6Hmo2T1&sig=5BD3odQYTC5R9nxgEBWKX_2OZHg&hl=en&sa=X&ei=IA1qVPegLMaeyASMuoDQBw&ved=0CCoQ6AEwBA#v=onepage&q=%22Safe%20in%20ourselves%2C%20while%20on%20ourselves%20we%20stand%22&f=false (accessed November 17, 2014).

Historical Archaeology in Georgia. 2004. Forest Park, GA: Georgia Dept. of Transportation, Office of Materials & Research.

Hochschild, Adam. 2005. *Bury the Chains*. Boston: Houghton Mifflin.

Holbrook, Stewart H. *Yankee Loggers: A Recollection of Woodsmen Cooks, and River Drivers*.

Johnson, Charles R. and Patricia Smith. 1998. *Africans in America: America's Journey Through Slavery*. New York: Harcourt Brace.

Johnstone, J. H. L. 1930. The Acadian-Newfoundland Earthquake of November 18, 1929. *Transactions of the Nova Scotia Institute of Science*, 17 (4): 227-37.

Joltes, Richard. N.d. *History, Hoax, and Hype – The Oak Island Legend*. http://www.criticalenquiry.org/oakisland/OI_myths.shtml (accessed August 2006).

Joseph, J.W., Theresa M. Hamby and Catherine S. Long. 2004. *Historical Archaeology in Georgia*. Forest Park, GA: Georgia Dept. of Transportation, Office of Materials & Research.

Knittle, Walter Allen. 1937. *Early Eighteenth Century Palatine Emigration*. Philadelphia: Dorance and Company.

Konig, David Thomas, ed. 1995. *Devising Liberty: Preserving and Creating Freedom in the New American Republic*. Stanford, CA: Stanford University Press.

Lescarbot, Marc and Henry P. Biggar. 1928. *Nova Francia, or a Description of Acadia*. New York: George Routledge.

Leslie, Alexander, ed. 2010. *Encyclopedia of African American History*. Santa Barbra: ABC-Clio, LLC.

Longstreth, Morris T. 1935. *To Nova Scotia*. Toronto: The Ryerson Press.

MacKay, Charles. 1841. *Memoirs of Extraordinary Popular Delusions*, vol. 1. London: Richard Bentley.

MacNutt, W. S. 1965. *The Atlantic Provinces*. Toronto: McClelland and Stewart.

MacPherson, David. 1805. *Annals of Commerce, Manufactures, Fisheries, and Navigation*, vol. 3. London: n.p.

Mahon, Lord. 1841. *History of England*, vol. I, 3rd ed. rev., Paris: Fain and Thunot.

Malone, Joseph J. 1979. *Pine Trees and Politics*: The Naval Stores and Forest Policy in Colonial New England 1691-1775. Seattle: University of Washington Press.

Manning, Samuel F. 1979. *New England Masts and the King's Broad Arrow*. Somerset, NH: Self-published.

Mayo, Lawrence Shaw. 1921. *John Wentworth, Governor of New Hampshire 1767-1775*. Cambridge, MA: Harvard University Press.

McCarthy, Justin Huntly. 1884. *A History of the Four Georges*, vol. 1, London: Chatto and Windus.

Morell, Virginia. 1983. "The Pit and the Perplexities." *Equinox*, May-June.

Mossman, Bob. 1981. "No Treasure, just Family Papers, says County Resident." *Bridgewater Bulletin*, August 12.

Oak Island Treasure Company Capital – Sixty Thousand Dollars. 1893. Brockton: Mandeville and Co. Printers.

O'Brien, John O. 2014. *Oak Island Unearthed! A Miner's Investigation into the Enigma of Oak Island, the Mesoamericans, and the Treasures Buried Therein*. Halifax, NS: New World Publishing.

O'Connor, Darcy. 2004. *The Secret Treasure of Oak Island: The Amazing True Story of a Centuries-Old Treasure Hunt*. Guilford, CT: The Lyons Press.

O'Farrell, John. 2007. An Utterly Impartial History of Britain – Or 2000 Years of Upper Class Idiots In Charge. London: Transworld Publishers.

Outland, Robert B., III. 2004. *Tapping the Pines: The Naval Stores Industry in the American South*. Baton Rouge, LA: Louisiana State University Press.

Porter, Andrew. 2004. *Religion Verses Empire*. Manchester, U.K.: Manchester University Press.

Preston, Douglas. 1988. Death Trap Defies Treasure Seekers for Two Centuries. *Smithsonian Magazine*, June.

Realey, Charles Bechdolt. 1935. *The London Journal and its Authors, 1720-1723* (Bulletin of the University of Kansas). December 1, 1935, vol. 36, no. 23.

Report on Canadian Archives. 1896. "Nova Scotia," 37. Ottawa: Queen's Printer.

Skinner, Jon S., ed. 1849. The Tar and Turpentine Business of North Carolina. *The Farmer's Library and Monthly Journal of Agriculture*, vol. II, 17. New York: Greely and McElrath.

Snow, Edward Rowe. 1951. *True Tales of Buried Treasure.* New York: Dodd, Mead and Co.

Sora, Steven. 1999. *The Lost Treasure of the Knights Templar: Solving the Oak Island Mystery.* Rochester, VT: Destiny Books.

The South Sea Bubble, and the Numerous Fraudulent Projects to Which it Gave Rise in 1720, 1825. 2nd ed. London: Thomas Boyd.

South, Stanley A. 2002. *Archaeological Pathways to Historic Site Development.* New York: Kluwer Academic/Plenum Publishers.

Stephenson, Robert L., ed. 1974. *The Institute of Archaeology Notebook* – University of South Carolina, vol. 6, Jan-Feb, 8-9.

Stow, John and John Mottley. 1735. *A Survey of the Cities of London and Westminster and Borough of Southwark and Parts Adjacent.* London: n.p.

"Tar-making in Bothnia." 1836. *The Penny Magazine of the Society for the Diffusion of Useful Knowledge*, vol. V, no. 247.

Waite, P. B. 1994. *The Lives of Dalhousie University: 1818-1925, Lord Dalhousie's College*, Montreal: McGill-Queen's University Press.

Waller, George Macgregor. 1960. *Samuel Vetch, Colonial Enterpriser.* Chapel Hill, NC: North Carolina Press.

Ward, Jay. 1949. Naval Stores: The Industry. *Trees: Yearbook of Agriculture.* United States Department of Agriculture.

Webster, John Clarence. 1934. *Acadia at the End of the Seventeenth Century.* The New Brunswick Museum.

West, John. 1827. *A Journal of a Mission to the Indians of the British Provinces.* London: L. B. Seeley and Son.

"What is Liquefaction?" Geology.com. http://geology.com/usgs/liquefaction/.

Windsor, Justin. 1887. *Narrative and Critical History of America: The English and French in North America 1689-1763*, vol. 5, Part 2. Boston and New York: The Riverside Press, Cambridge.